Paganism

The Complete Guide to Nature-based Spirituality for Every New Seeker

(Learn and Apply the Practice of Nature-based Spirituality)

Jesse Wheeler

Published By **Ryan Princeton**

Jesse Wheeler

Paganism: The Complete Guide to Nature-based Spirituality for Every New Seeker (Learn and Apply the Practice of Nature-based Spirituality)

ISBN 978-1-998901-72-2

No part of this guidbook shall be reproduced in any form without permission in writing from the publisher except in the case of brief quotations embodied in critical articles or reviews.

Legal & Disclaimer

The information contained in this book is not designed to replace or take the place of any form of medicine or professional medical advice. The information in this book has been provided for educational & entertainment purposes only.

The information contained in this book has been compiled from sources deemed reliable, and it is accurate to the best of the Author's knowledge; however, the Author cannot guarantee its accuracy and validity and cannot be held liable for any errors or omissions. Changes are periodically made to this book. You must consult your doctor or get professional medical advice before using any of the suggested remedies, techniques, or information in this book.

Table of Contents

Chapter 1: The Creation

Norse mythology is characterized by a distinct beginning and a clear end. It begins with the story of creation. It ends with Ragnarok which is the final chapter of the world, as well as the demise of many mortals and gods. Before we can reach the end, it is important to know the beginning.

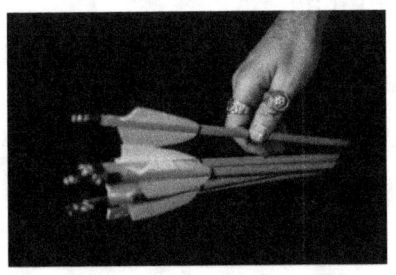

Before anything existed in the world, the universe was in a state of nonexistence. The world of Norse mythology began with Ginnungagap, a void that predated land, sea or sky. Ginnungagap was a quiet and deep abyss, prophesied to return later in Ragnarok. This dark and bleak period can be described within the Poetic Edda, specifically in the poem Voluspa which reads:

"That was the time when no thing was.

There was no sand neither sea, nor cool waves.

There is no sky, earth, or grass,

Only Ginnungagap"

Ginnungagap was situated in the middle that was between the world of flame Muspelheim which was incredibly hot and rife with smoke and molten lava and the realm of the ice Niflheim in which there was only fog and thick frost. These elements were strong and relentless, and they each was able to spread out in a wildly. In the midst of fires, Muspelheim and ice was forming out of Niflheim and then the two clashed at Ginnungagap. The clash of these two powerful elements caused chaos and the fire even managed to melt the ice. From the droplets of melt ice Ymir was born - the very first giant (jotuns) with both female and male reproductive organs that could reproduce sexually.

Ymir wasn't the only creature made from melting drops. Audhumla (Audumbla) was the first cow of the era was also created. The milk of Audumbla nourished Ymir. While Ymir was asleep, sweat that he shed from his armpits birthed two females and a male. The giants grew out of his legs as well - the son of six heads is believed to have emerged from the left leg of Ymir.

The cow ate Ymir and helped keep alive with four streams of milk flowing from her teats. How did the cow remain alive? The answer to this question can be found by the Prose Edda, where it is revealed that Audumbla was a lover of salty rime stones as a source of sustenance and led to the birth of gods with names we're still familiar with.

The first night that Audumbla had licked the rime stones in order to nourish her hair, a man's became visible to the woman while she licked. Later, in the following days the head and body were revealed through the frozen. Buri is the founder of the Aesir gods, and had a son named Bor (Borr). The method by which Bor was created is not known however we do are aware that Bor got married to Bestla (the daughter of Bolthorn (the giant Bolthorn) as well Odin, Vili, and Ve were born of the union.

They were half-giants, part god, and they were able to create the world. Odin, Vili, and Ve would like to be gods and rule the world, however, they required a world to build the world they needed basic material. To accomplish this, their three brother killed Ymir and transported his body to the center of the abyss known as Ginnungagap. They created the universe from his body. The blood of Ymir was so thick that it was able to flood the earth and formed oceans. The muscles and skin created the soil, while Ymir's breath filled the soil with plants. The brain of Ymir created the clouds. The bones of Ymir formed stones and rocks.

They took Ymir's skull , and placed it on the earth, creating the sky. Four dwarfs were charged with carrying the sky/skull: Nordi, Sudri, Austri and Vestri each one of which corresponds to the cardinal direction of east, north, south and west. Muspelheim was often referred to as Muspell is still in burning with flames, and three brothers used to use them. They took sparks and burning embers and threw them into the void , to provide us with the light and stars. The brothers gave the stars the freedom to move around within.

When Ymir passed away his body started to decay and, out of the decaying flesh, worms began to grow and this is how Dwarves were born. The moment the Aesir gods were aware of them, they saw that they had potential, and they gave them a sense of intelligence. This is explained in the poem that opens the Prose Edda called Gylfaginning:

"Then all the gods of power left

to the thrones of destiny,

the most sacred gods and

they came up with a consensus to discuss the matter

A troop of dwarfs

need to be created

from the bloody waves

and the limbs of Brimir (another alternative name to Ymir)

Men's similarity is evident.

They were made many

Dwarves are dwarves living in the earth.

as Durin as Durin." As Durin stated. Gylfaginning

The dwarves became skilled craftsmen and were responsible for the creation of many of the greatest weapons around including Thor's hammer as well as fine jewelry and other objects. When dwarves emerged from Ymir's body , and the four brothers were sent to lift the sky and stop it from falling and falling, the remaining dwarves settled down in caves and rocks which is which is also known as Svartalfheim which is the homeworld of the dwarfs.

The Sun and Moon

The Edda describes the way in which the moon and the sun became a reality, named for two gods called Sol (the female) and Mani (the male). Old Norse for 'sun, in addition to Mani (the male) meaning moon. The tale of how they were able to control the day and night for the Vikings isn't clear and there are various theories about it.

According to one account it is said that the two were the daughters and sons of an Midgard man called Mundilfari who was extremely proud of his children that he named them children the sun and moon. He would claim that they were as beautiful as gods themselves which upset the gods for a mortal to boast about his creation in such a way that he would give his children names that were powerful.

Thus, the gods grabbed Sol as well as Mani and put them into the heavens to control the cycles of day and night. Sol is the driver of the sun chariot, and guides the two horses that pull them, though she did not perform it on her own volition. Sol was required to steer her chariot quickly since she was pursued by a wolf known as Skoll who would hunt his prey and eat her in one night. In contrast, Mani guided the moon and controlled its cycles of wax and waning. Mani was hunted by moon hounds referred to as Hati (hate) as well as Skoll (treachery) which would devour Mani each day, but the moon beats them out and has the ability to heal itself. As with the other sister of his, Mani was eventually consumed by his warg wolf hunter in Ragnarok which meant the day and night would be gone forever.

Within the Prose Edda, Sol rides with a character named Svalinn who is armed with an imposing shield that protects Midgard and humankind from the burning glare from the sun.

The Creation of Humans

Contrary to Prometheus who made man out of mud Odin, Vili, and Ve invented the first human and woman from tree trunks. They named the three Ask as well as Embla. The story behind their birth. After killing his father and creating the world from the corpse of his father, Odin was out enjoying his work and strolling along the shores in one of these newly formed waters or the oceans. Two brothers were there in his midst, although another version states that gods from gods from other religions were

also with him.

While walking through the sand, they came across two tree trunks that were floating onto the beach. These two wood pieces resembled like human beings that was a man and one woman, but they were lifeless and motionless. That was the time when the gods made the decision to give an opportunity for life these pieces of wood to make real human beings.

Odin is the person who put life into the fragments of wood. Vili and Ve provided them with the capacity and mental acuity that allowed them to hear speak, talk, and see as well as have a healthy, glowing complexion. The two also gave us Odr which is an Old Norse concept that means divine inspiration, also known as what we call imagination or the ability to develop ideas. This is the power that drives and drives us to do and think. Our connection to God whatever it is can be, propels us forward and drives us to pursue higher levels of knowledge.

The gods gave names to two gods, the male Ask and female Embla and they were granted a place to call Midgard which is the realm of humans. Midgard was bolstered by eyelashes of Ymir to shield humans from the wrath of the giants that were dangerous and angry, according to what the mythology suggested. Ask And Embla are the humans' parents according to Norse mythology. Ask is derived in Ask, which is the Old Norse word 'Askr, which means "ash tree. Embla's name is more complex and is interpreted differently by the scholars.

The information we have on the beginning of the development of humans being are not complete, and they move from telling tales of dwarves and meanders on to the human creation. Experts believe that the sequence and order that are in Poetic Edda verses that culminate in the creation of two first humans suggest that the Dwarves, master craftsmen who created human-like figures from the wood that gods found and breathed into.

The Giants' Fate

The creation myth in Norse mythology may suggest that giants are a caste or lesser gods than the gods, but this is not the case. Giants (Jotunn) (or giants) (Jotnar) have the same ancestry as all gods. Odin himself is directly descendant of the giants and, consequently and so are all the gods who follow him, whether directly or indirectly in their descent through Thor up to Freya.

Giants are always associated with chaos and destruction that is reflected by their name. The word "Jotunn" translates to 'devourer' as well as other variations of their names have not less terrifying interpretations. The name Ymir was translated into "screamer. The offspring of Ymir was the product of chaos, just as his parents were a result of the chaos of the world before the creation.

This is the reason why the gods look like the opposite of the giants from Norse mythology. The idea isn't to say that giants are evil and the gods good however, rather that they were two opposing forces that came in the same spot. The reason for this idea is that gods were associated with the creation (humans seas, skies, seas as well as the sky.) while the giants were related to destruction.

The majority of giants were drowned by the blood of Ymir, which killed the majority of his children and Jotnar would have died out had Bergelmir not escaped along with his wife. The two giants escaped through the use of a Ludr (a blowing sound made by a horn) and in tandem they brought back the giant race, and also parented the giants of frost. We'll get into more details on the giants as well as their future home however, for now, it is important to be aware that mortals were shielded from the fury and devastation of the new race of giants living in Midgard with the fencing made from the

eyelashes of Ymir.

If we take a look more closely to this Norse myth of creation we'll discover that it is deeply rooted in human nature. The empty Ginnungagap as well as the gigantic Ymir are both an expression of chaos and could be seen as a representation of the immense unknown that the Vikings could have feared. This chaos may also speak of the limitless potential humanity has if only be shown the right way and directed towards the proper direction. The gods made a existence and its people from the chaos.

That's why the giants are a symbol of chaos. They were born from Ymir the son of his offspring and the gods created mortals, whether for good or worse. For as long as humans and giants exist, humankind will think of the giants as harbinger of doom and agents for chaos, since it's the blood of their species. They believed in the Vikings believed that giants would eventually accomplish their aim and take over the gods at the time Ragnarok arrived.

Another method of looking at the relationship between gods and the giants is how gods steal resources from giants in order to create things for themselves, beginning with Ymir. The materials taken by gods are of diverse nature and are an array of not only craft elements but also the capacity to think.

Chaos and Creation in Viking Culture

The Vikings were warriors and it's no surprise that the story of creation is a saga of destruction, chaos and change in their society. Creation mythology is a source of death and conflict and people of the Germanic people, as a whole were usually in a state of war and had an immense satisfaction in killing their foes. This war that causes the Germanic people is not only between their gods Gods and giants but as well among the elements that comprised ice and fire which created the world as we see it now.

The way in which the murder of Ymir is depicted as part of Norse mythology is as well presented in a manner distinct from other murders of various religions, such as Cain as well as Abel. The gods did not commit a sin by killing Ymir. They were doing something that was necessary, beneficial even. This is evident by the Germanic people's perception of death and war. While they were not calling for unnecessary bloodshed or insanity-inducing killing, they believed that embracing war and life was often a necessity or even a sacred obligation. There are those who say the way of life of the Vikings was warlike, full of determination, strength and unstoppable determination. They put up a fight for courage and fame and they were never slowing their progress.

Also in the case of the Vikings they were often able to find honor in certain kinds of violence and war, much like there was respect when Odin along with his brothers.' killing of Ymir. This was the most significant job that anyone has ever done and was the catalyst for the creation for the modern world.

Chapter 2: The Cosmos in Norse Mythology

The universe of the Germanic people, and specifically the Vikings were comprised of nine worlds on which different species lived. We know very little about the nine realms because they aren't mentioned in any myths, particularly regarding their position within the World Tree of Yggdrasil. Also, the illustrations that show Midgard or any other world in particular locations within the tree of the universe are mostly speculation and theories.

In reality the nine worlds often discussed when discussing Norse mythology are all based upon some theories. While the nine worlds appear in the Edda however, there is no indication of which of the worlds comprise the nine. Therefore, a speculative view offers us the nine worlds we have from the race we know through Norse mythology.

We'll go into the specific worlds in the near future in the near future, but for now, they're:

* Midgard: The realm of the mortals in which humans lived.

* Vanaheim the world in which Vanaheim was the place where Vanir goddesses and gods resided.

* Asgard The world of home for The Aesir Gods and Goddesses.

* Muspelheim The primordial realm of fire and flames.

* Niflheim The primordial realm of ice and frost.

* Jotunheim The world of the giants in the frost.

* Nidavellir or Svartalfheim The homeworld of the dwarfs.

* Alfheim The home of the light elves. world.

* Hel or Helheim The underworld, controlled by Hel.

Midgard has been identified as being the one one of the nine linked to Yggdrasil and believed that it is visible rendering the rest inaccessible. But, they may be seen or explored from the outside world as Jotunheim that is connected to the physical world's wilderness and the underworld of Hel accessible through the grave. Asgard also shares a common space with the skies of the visible world.

When you are studying the worlds of nine, one aspect to remember what is significant about the numeral itself, that clearly had spiritual significance in those of Germanic people. This is demonstrated in more than only the division of the universe into nine different worlds. For example, Odin sacrificed himself by hanging for nine days and nine nights in Yggdrasil to seek knowledge. There are numerous other stories of Norse myths and legends in which numbers nine play an important part. According to scholars such as Rudolf Simek, this could be a result of the lunar calendar in which 27 days is a multiple of nine.

Yggdrasil

Yggdrasil is the tree of life which connects the worlds of Norse mythology. It was born from the primordial void Ginnungagap to link the realms of nine, and its branches link the whole universe. This means that the security of the universe is contingent on the tree. Yggdrasil is the glue that holds the universe together and its roots bind the worlds of nine.

Diverse and sometimes contradictory sources examine the amount of branches and roots for Yggdrasil. Some believe they believe that the branches that make up Yggdrasil reach into the heavens to the point that they tower above the clouds. The summit is covered with snow as high as the most awe-inspiring of mountains, and is surrounded by powerful winds at that high altitude.

The roots of Yggdrasil extend through three deep wells, Urdarbrunnr, Mimisbrunnr, and Hvergelmir. Three wells, or springs are located beneath the tree and go to three distinct and distant areas. The theory proposed by Snorri Sturluson suggests that there are three root systems for the tree, with one root in each well.

The belief is it is true that Urdarbrunnr is not beneath Yggdrasil. The well is located in the sky in the heavens, where gods hold regular councils to discuss matters that affect the entire world. Hvergelmir is deep under the second root, which goes down to Niflheim which is the land filled with frost and ice. It's this particular root that the dragons eat. Mimisbrunnr is an underground well that transports branches from the life tree up to Jotunheim and is linked to the knowledgeable Mimir.

In addition, these sources are said to spread out to the underworld , which nobody could even see prior to their death, not even the shamans.

The roots of the name Yggdrasil are related to Odin, the god of Odin himself. "Yggr" is a reference to "terrible or the terrifier it was among the numerous names Odin was famously known as and a testimony to the ferocity Odin had been to Germanic people. "Drasil," on other hand, translates to "horse," and we could translate the meaning of the tree of life as 'the the horse that was Odin. The Germanic populace believed Yggdrasil could be an ash-tree, but various versions and variants of the myth assert that the species was not known.

Many animals are linked to Yggdrasil with some being symbolically more than the others. A number of stags, including Dvalinn, Dainn, Duneyrr and Durathror consume the tree continuously, and it is the living tree that is constantly recuperating as well as replenishing its. At the foot of Yggdrasil there are dragons, or serpents are buried, beginning by the dragon Nidhogg who chews on the roots of the tree. This dangerous practice can cause harm to trees that hold the universe together. This is the reason Nidhogg is believed by some to play an important role in Ragnarok and how his actions may trigger the tree's shaking, signalling the beginning of the end of.

At the highest point of Yggdrasil an eagle that has no name is residing with its wings flapping, bring about the wind that we encounter in our everyday world. A squirrel named Ratatoskr leaps around the tree in order to relay messages between the dragon and the eagle, and in reverse, mostly news and insults. Three roosters are singing under the canopy of the tree looking around and one known as Gullinkambi will croak most loudly when Ragnarok arrives on the planet sending a signal to the entire universe that the end of the world is near.

The significance of these animals is open to interpretation, and a lot of researchers have debated theories throughout the years. Many think that the dragons and the serpents devouring the roots of the tree, which compromises the stability of the tree, symbolises the Yggdrasil's death and as a result the universe's. It's a signal that life is fleeting It's not just the gods and mortals who remain for a brief time period as well as the cosmic system itself. The Germanic people believed in the supernatural and fought with courage. Maybe they did this because they were aware how short their lives on earth was short and should be spent fighting valiantly and dying in honor.

Despite the absence of maps or graphs illustrating the nine realms surrounding Yggdrasil The scholars have consulted the existing sources to formulate what they believe to be the way Germanic people perceived the nine realms as they relate to the living tree. The belief is that the world may be arranged according to two axes, one horizontal and one vertical. If we suppose the vertical axis runs parallel to the trunk of Yggdrasil Then Asgard would be situated on the top branch, while Hel at the foot of its roots. Midgard is then in the ground at the bottom of Yggdrasil.

Horizontal axis also had a characteristic that Vikings made for worlds depending on whether or not they were civilized, something will be discussed in a minute. In the meantime, we'll have to look more deeply at the way in which Germanic people saw Yggdrasil as a source of life everywhere which connects not just the nine realms, or worlds together, but also the universe as a whole, while preserving its structure and the regularity that we are familiar with.

The Norns and Yggdrasil

They Norns had a powerful feminine characters who symbolized the concept of fate or time in different forms and were among the most, if not the most fearsome beings from all of Norse mythology. Every person was dependent on fate, including the gods and goddesses which meant that Norns were revered and feared.

Three Norns looked after Yggdrasil to keep it alive and making sure it was healthy and strong to protect the universe. Verdandi, Skuld, and Urdr. The fates of these Norns resided in a room next to the water source of Urdarbrunnr and drank the water. Each day they would pour the water over the life-giving tree to ensure that it was kept green. If they do not complete their job, the roots will begin to decay, and the tree would soon follow.

The Norns utilize water from Urdarbrunnr due to the belief that the water from this well holds magical properties that can transform everything it touches into white, with the exception of the life-giving tree Yggdrasil itself. One of the most well-known myths surrounding Yggdrasil as well as the Norns is the story of Odin's sacrifice on his search for knowledge and how he was able to lose his eyesight and acquire that distinctive appearance, which is illustrated by numerous paintings over the decades.

The Norns' roles and the care they provide for Yggdrasil should not be overlooked. The Norns' role has a more profound significance to the fact that the tree requires to be treated with care and affection. The tree of life, sacred to all of us, on which the security of the universe rests is much more than a mere mortal. It's like a living thing that requires protection and love to thrive, as when it falls and dies, the entire world of gods and mortals is swept away with it. Odin was a speaker regarding Yggdrasil within The Poetic Edda, saying that it suffers more pain than most people can comprehend A stag nibbles at it from above, but at its back, it's rotting and Nidhogg breaks it to pieces beneath.'

The Nine Worlds

1. Asgard

One of the first nine realms we'll discuss is Asgard which is home to the Aesir gods. It is perhaps one of the biggest among the realms. Asgard has been prominent in pop culture through movies and comics throughout time however, it meant much for the Germanic people long before that. Asgard was home to gods of war, and also a source of hope and light and civilization. Asgard was only accessible via the Bifrost - which was a bridge of rainbows connecting Asgard to Midgard and other realms.

Asgard is believed to have been divided into 12 or additional realms and each of the major Aesir gods residing in one of these realms. They resided in castles of silver and gold, fitting for the gods of the past. A lot of Germanic citizens believed nobles of their day were in residences that were similar to ones of Aesir gods of Asgard.

The most significant among the twelve realms in Asgard was Valhalla The hall of Odin the god of all Gods and where warriors who had been killed were able to live peacefully. In Valhalla the brave warriors who were killed in battle eat boars killed each day, and consume the spirits of goats. They battle each other each day to play sports and entertainment. At night, they are restored from any injuries they may have suffered.

Valhalla is an intriguing place in Norse mythology. It is the last resting place for brave warriors who will reside there until Ragnarok because, at that point they will become Odin's army. If Ragnarok comes around, and the Twilight of the Gods is on the horizon These fallen warriors will rise. They will march out of Odin's hall and through the 540 gates of the palace. They will battle the giants alongside their chieftain.

Thor's Hall in Asgard was named Bilskirnir It was described as being one of the largest and magnificent in the entire region of Asgard. Thor's hall was believed to be situated in the vast area of Thrudheim. Similar to Valhalla the mansion contained more than 500 rooms which could have been located in Valhalla or in other locations across the vast landscape that comprise Thrudheim. Aesir world.

On Asgard there was a second area where the majority of brave warriors that died in battle were taken to Freyja's field was known as Folkvangr. There are a variety of sources on how warriors were chosen to go either to Valhalla as well as Folkvangr. Some believe that Freyja chose her portion of the dead prior to Odin however it's not entirely 100% certain, particularly considering how well documented Valhalla is in mythology, even more than Folkvangr. Breidablik was Baldur's residence on Asgard It was described as being almost divine with its cleanliness and beauty that nobody evil or filthy could live there.

Asgard was a place with the highest fertility of any ever before and was home to many precious stones and riches. A tall wall of stone protected Asgard and was believed to be unfinished due to the fact that Thor destroyed the person who built it, Hrimthurs, a giant disguised as an architect. The builder demanded the bride's hand as well as the moon and sun to pay to perform his work. The gods were unaware that they were a gigantic in disguise, and offered him what they believed was an impossible task building the walls surrounding Asgard within six months. There was no money in the event that the builder failed to complete the job by then.

Surprised The gods discovered that their builder as well as his horse Svadilfari were making progress more quickly than they had anticipated. There were a few days left until the deadline of six months was over and the builder and Svadilfari's horse were almost completed with the wall. That's the time that Loki dressed himself up as a mare to was able to lure Svadilfari off the wall in order that the builder wouldn't be held. This worked. The builder sprinted following his horse, and the latter ran after the mare. Snorri Sturluson states that in Prose Edda:

"And the next evening when the builder set out in search of stone on his horse Svadilfare the mare abruptly fled from the woods towards the horse, and started to yell at him. The horse, having a clue as to the kind of horse this was, became enthralled and broke the reins and chased the horse, who fled from him into the forest. The builder raced after them with all of his power and hoped to catch the horse, but the horses continued to run all night and the time passed and, at dawn the work had not been able to progress as usual."

-Gylfaginning

The wall wasn't completed in time, so gods were not required to pay for the giant such an exorbitant cost. The gods stumbled upon it was actually a gigantic disguised in the form of a giant they enlisted the help of Thor to kill the giant by crushing his skull by hammering him with Mjollnir.

Asgard is in the sky of the Germanic people, but there are some theories that believe it to represent more of a spiritual than physical place. Important issues were settled within the plains of Idavoll in the middle at the heart of Asgard in the middle of Asgard, where the gods gathered in the grand hall of Gladsheim as the goddesses gathered at the Hall at Vingolf for discussions about the future of human beings as well as other gods as well. The less important issues were left to fates of the

Norns. The gods also congregated within the wells of Urd beneath the Yggdrasil's Asgard root.

Despite the magic that flowed through Asgard as well as the reality that goddesses and gods resided in the area, Asgard was very much similar to Midgard the realm of the human. They had magnificent castles and lush fields, but they were built using the same materials and featured the same animals and plants. If they had been to Asgard It wouldn't be like home to the majority of humans. Asgard was larger and its land was larger and more beautiful, however it was a close kinship with the world of the mortals for the most part. But humans didn't possess the capability of traveling to Asgard because the ability to travel between realms was not common at first, and was not an easy feat even for gods.

The gods also created the Bifrost and the travelling between realms became little more simple. When a god wanted for a journey to Midgard then they would travel across the rainbow bridge and enter the realm of mortals. According to legend, gods traveled across the Bifrost each day to commune in the well beneath Yggdrasil. Humans, however were not able to enjoy this luxury and could not travel freely to Asgard. Many could glimpse Bifrost once or twice but locating its exact location and where it went down was difficult because the bridge wasn't designed for humans.

Asgard is often linked Vanaheim which was the home of Vanaheim, the home of Vanir Gods and Goddesses, with Midgard. The Vanir did not have a directly connected connection with Midgard as did that of the Bifrost on Asgard as a result, in order to go to the realm of mortals it was necessary to go to Asgard and travel from there. The Bifrost was guarded to keep any unwanted visitors from sneaking in to the gods of Asgard. The Bifrost was guarded by a god known as Heimdall who watched carefully over it and made sure that nobody was able to travel through Midgard towards Asgard. Near the outskirts of Asgard was Himinbjorg which was Heimdall's home. It was near the Bifrost which was where Heimdall could keep an of the bridge.

According to one interpretation of the legend Asgard's final battle would occur in Ragnarok when the forces of Muspelheim would advance on Asgard through the Bifrost. Heimdall would blow his hornto signal as the start of the ending. Some versions of the tale suggest that Bifrost will crumble due to the force of the giants of fire that were swarming around Muspelheim However, this does not agree with other versions. We do know that the war will continue to rage over Midgard as well. Asgard could be destroyed in the process that shows how interconnected to each other both realms are, since the demise that is happening to the realms of death can impact the Aesir world in a huge way.

It is important to remember that there is no account in Norse myths about the way Asgard was constructed. As opposed to Midgard The myths that have been passed to us don't describe how the land was built by the Aesir gods was built however, scholars have tried over time to develop theories that are compatible with the stories we have. Some even go to the extent of linking the origins of Norse gods with Greek people such as the King Priam and King Priam of Troy.

2. Midgard

Midgard is the realm that contains more stories and myths from Norse mythology, more than Asgard. As we've said earlier, Midgard was the only among the realms that was predominantly in the world of visible and was not connected to other realms that were usually invisible. Midgard was a middle world that was advanced and civilized and the word roughly translates to "civilization. But there were other meanings which were in line with this that described or referred to the mortal realm a "civilization" located in the middle of the wild world, populated with creatures of the night and monsters. Midgard was also a part of the other realms, which was surrounded by an ocean of danger that was inaccessible and a huge serpent that was capable of devouring the entire world.

On the other hand Midgard was located in Jotunheim with its giants of frost as if an ocean surrounded an island or continent. Jormungandr, the world serpent Jormungandr is also a part of the mortal realm , and dwells in the ocean alongside other creatures such as Aegir as well as Ran. Jormungandr is the symbol of the treacherous sea which takes numerous unwitting travellers. On the other the other hand there's Asgard as the symbol of order and civilization. In a sense, Midgard is the center of the universe for Germanic people, and is the place where you can distinguish those who are civilized from those who are not. It is, in actual the place where contemporary fantasy writers such as Tolkien came up with the name "Middle Earth" via Norse myths. The term Midgard can also translate to mean'middle yard..'

But, Midgard had its fair amount of chaos, despite being part of the civilization. Mortals have their own side of them, and they tend to blur the lines between order and chaos similar to how Midgard is a place that straddles the worlds of both ideals. But, Midgard strives to be more civil and lawful as Asgard and not uncivilized as Jotunheim.

The inhabitants of Midgard were prone to attack and required protection. This was the wall made out of Ymir's eyelashes keep out the Jotnar. The Midgard world Midgard was safe but was accessible to other species like elves and dwarfs However, the decision to leave Midgard however was a different matter. Humans could not cross the ocean to get to the wall that protected them, even though some might have attempted to do so.

Midgard was in the hands of Thor the Odin's protector with Odin as the Allfather watching over his creations using his ravens. As we've mentioned before, Ragnarok would take place in Midgard and the entire world would be devastated, and the entire world would be swept away in the waters. The people would look at the signs of war - three winters and no summers will befall the world and wars would rage. People will be fighting, and family members are likely to turn against one another, abandoning the bonds of family and affection. The moon and the sun would disappear, and the ground will shake violently.

The world serpent will rise to infect the air. His gigantic body will create massive waves that will flood across the entire earth, degrading everything that crosses their way. However, a new earth will emerge from the sea in the end, and a new day of peace will be born. There are a lot of similarities between this account of events and Christianity and Christianity, possibly because of the role played by the Germanic people through Christianity that occurred later in the ages.

Myths and legends morphed, and, along with Christian influence, led to a new era over the course of. In the old Norse myths and stories, Ragnarok would end with the destruction of Asgard and Midgard and the demise of gods. It was not a time of new age and Midgard did not be able to rise from its underworld tomb. Maybe this latest version of Ragnarok was the Germanic people's way of dealing with the terror of the unknown which came after the death of. It's true that a tale of destruction and destruction that destroys the entire world with no hope of a new beginning or a new era is quite frightening and is also quite distinct from other tales of doom across various religions, where there is always the possibility of a new beginning following the conclusion.

3. Vanaheim

Vanaheim can be described as the second among nine worlds in which gods reside However, only the gods of Vanir are the ones who reside there and in contrast to the Aesir. We'll talk about the differences in those of the Aesir as well as the Vanir gods, and their battle that ended in peace. However, for now, we will concentrate on Vanaheim which is Vanir's home world. The exact location of Vanaheim is not known and there are no reliable sources to confirm the exact location of Vanaheim in Yggdrasil. A poem from the Poetic Edda talks of one of the Vanir gods who traveled eastward towards Asgard during the conflict between gods from both tribes that might lead us to believe that Vanaheim is located west of Asgard.

While some scholars have attributed the origins of the name "Vanaheim" in the hands of Icelandic poet Snorri Sturluson actually an Old Norse source that mentions the name Vanaheim and suggests that it existed prior to Snorri's time. However, as you'll see it is a bit difficult to find information and we don't know anything about Vanaheim apart from the fact that it was home to Vanir. Vanir.

It is believed that the Vanir gods were closely associated with nature, in contrast to the god Aesir gods, who were associated with order, wisdom, along with social stability. This might suggest that Vanaheim was an untamed place or uncivilized, at the very least, when compared to the way Midgard as well as Asgard are depicted in Norse myths. This could be the reason Asgard was of more significance in Norse mythology, and is frequently mentioned more often than Asgard, and with the more powerful gods and goddesses residing in the area.

It's a good opportunity to look at one of the ways in which the Germanic people made distinctions between geographical spaces/lands and mental states. This is due to the way they described their lands and worlds which ended with "gard" as opposed to "heim. You'll notice that the worlds that are civilized are characterized by 'gard', such as Asgard and Midgard and the more wild ones end with "heim," such as Muspelheim as well as Niflheim. The reasoning behind this could be supportive of the belief that Vanaheim was located on the wilder side and wasn't as civilized, or did not have the same social system like Midgard or Asgard.

The Vanir Gods and Goddesses who were associated with Vanaheim prior to the conflict were from nature and the wilderness, rather than wisdom and war, as was the case with the Aesir. Freyja is the god of love, fertility and magic. Her sister

Freyr was god of rain, fertility, and sun. Njord was god of sea and wind.

It is not clear what the description is for Vanaheim however, the legend says that it must be green and pleasant similar to Asgard in which abundance and fertility abound. Vanaheim was full of beautiful light and beauty and the gods of Vanaheim were of harvests that were good and blessed their land with soft winds and wonderful weather.

4. Jotunheim

The next is Jotunheim The world of the giants of frost which is the foe of gods and mortals. Jotunheim is located at the far edge of the Germanic society's notion of what is considered to be barbaric or uncivilized. Jotunheim describes itself as a brutal world within the Eddas where winter is harsh and the weather is unstoppable. The forest is dark and sombre that extend for miles and mountains that are too cold for humans to endure. The home of the giants is dark and, luckily for the inhabitants of Midgard it was not visible as such a bleak world could have been too terrifying for ordinary people to see. Jotunheim was not a good place for humans to live in and the crops were not able to thrive in the area since there was neither fertile soil nor great weather.

Jotunheim was the home of giants of frost and rock and menacing creatures that menaced gods and mortals alike. Because of the harsh climate of the world and the plight of the giants living in Jotunheim were forced to survive on fishing and hunting, not harvesting. One thing that separates Jotunheim from Asgard and Midgard is the fact that Jotunheim's river does not freeze as if the Giants could strike at the Aesir and mortals too.

Thrym was the feared leader of Jotunheim who was known as the King of the Frost Giants and a terrifying character in Norse legends. Thrym was well-known to the Norse people as the monster who stole Thor's hammer and forced gods to grant his bride Freyja's hand. Utgard-Loki on the other on the other hand, was the stronghold of Utgard which was the largest and most powerful town in Jotunheim. There were other strongholds and cities throughout Jotunheim that were each was home to giants that played an integral part in the mythology of many. A lot of these giants, and especially Thor were in contacts with Aesir gods.

There are some scholars who believe that the Germanic people, specifically the Vikings were able to imagine Jotunheim as a place similar to their own. Jotunheim was a place that was a mess where the powerful lived, led by chieftains who ruled strongholds and would launch attacks whenever it was necessary. But, the realm of the frost giants was much larger size than the Vikings. Castles such as Utgard-Loki's were massive and had icicles that were so large that the tips of their icebergs could not be visible.

Giants of Jotunheim were constant thorns on the back of Aesir gods, causing chaos whenever they could and challenging gods many times. This is the reason Thor was entrusted with the task of protecting the human race as well as Asgard from the frenzied and turbulent giants. Yet giants and gods were not always at war. There was a variety of documented connections between the gods of Aesir as well as giants. Odin himself was Thor who was a giantess named Jord who was the goddess of the earth as it was. Odin's son Thor was in a relationship the giantess and she had two sons - Magni Modi and Magni. Modi.

Other gods who married giants include Freyr who got married to Gerd and also The Vanir god Njord got married to a giantess whose name was Skadi -which is also believed to be one of Odin's numerous lovers. The giants of Jotunheim were not always enemies of gods.

Numerous significant events occurred within Jotunheim as a part of Norse myths, including Odin giving up his eyes to gain wisdom, which we'll explore during this publication. Jotunheim was a key element in the folklore and myths that formed the Germanic people, not only for its significance as an antithesis to all which Asgard and Midgard was. Jotunheim was also a realm that the Vikings considered to be mirroring their own world, one in which it was difficult to survive, and there was a lot that had to be earned and not handed over.

5. Muspelheim

Muspelheim is the world of primordial of fire which existed at the very beginning of all things deep within the bowels of the vacuum. It's home to the giants of fire and a terrifying enemy that can cause a lot of destruction. The world is rife with hot lava and ash, with active volcanoes spreading across the entire land. Muspelheim was not a place in which gods, or even mortals could roam free. The fire-filled world was uninhabitable for people who weren't accustomed to the harsh environment. Only Odin could freely enter Muspelheim since he was considered to be the most intelligent and powerful god of all.

A lot of myths and legends of Germanic mythology are based on frost giants. A number of significant events happen in Jotunheim. The gods have had quite a number of encounters with frost giants. But, this isn't necessarily the case in Muspelheim. The fire realm appears to be a closed, unaccessible to anyone outside while the creatures believed to remain in and in a state of limbo, unable to escape. Fire giants are ruled by a demon who was a fire Surtr which is a central character in Norse mythology that is a key character in

Ragnarok. Surtr is the name given to him by Germanic populace believed Surtr was guarding Muspelheim and guarded the gates. However, the most plausible explanation is Surtr is trapped, and just waiting to see the gate be opened so the he can unleash his wrath on the gods and mortals alike.

As Ragnarok begins, Surtr will lead an army of giants in fire through the gate of Muspelheim and onwards to Asgard and will destroy Aesir. Aesir city. Surtr will take on the god Freyr and the two will fight in a bloody battle that will leave horrible trail of destruction in the wake of. It is important to note that Muspelheim is not exactly like the hell of Christianity as well as other religions. Although Muspelheim is home to a devilish figure and is a place of endless terrors as well as a fiery world but it's not the place where the dead are buried when they die. It is Helheim which is the underworld of the Germanic people who reside in Scandinavia.

One could argue both worlds maybe paired with Niflheim the other primordial world , but made of frost and ice, are the equivalent of hell in the modern world of religions.

6. Niflheim

Northern realms, Niflheim, is the most primordial of the worlds made of ice and fire protected by thick fog. It's a dark place which is also inaccessible and unhospitable to anyone else. As we've seen earlier, Niflheim together with Muspelheim was emerged from the Ginnungagap-like void and, together, they made one of the giants, Ymir which was the source from which the other gods and giants also were born.

Niflheim is also known as the home that is the tomb, the home of the wicked men who pass through Helheim in order to be shivering in the cold and darkness. Niflheim is under the control of Goddess Hel. The belief is the belief that Hel (the Underworld) was situated somewhere in Niflheim where, from the goddess Hel was the ruler of. In contrast to Valhalla which was where the brave could die, Niflheim was where the people who were not worthy would go to when they died.

There are many places in Niflheim including the most sinister of which is dedicated to the worst of humankind. For instance, Niflhel is in Helheim It's the lowest hell reserved for the most vile of the most evil. Certain versions of the myth also mention ice giants who resided in Niflheim However, the exact location of their residence was not known.

7. Alfheim

Alfheim is home to the elves, and specifically the light elves. That is the reason it's often called Ljosalfheim in certain sources. Alfheim is among the places we know little about. This could be the case for its inhabitants who are called those who are light-elves. Old Norse sources provide only a few details about this race, and the places they lived , despite representations of them in the popular press and other contemporary stories of the fantasy genre.

The limited information available about Alfheim informs us that it was the residence of Freyr the god Freyr and was where he built his home. There are some legends that claim Alfheim was gifted the city to Freyr as a "tooth gift gifts for infants given when their first teeth grew. If true, it could mean that Freyr was appointed the king of Alfheim as an infant, barely one or two months old.

One of the things we are aware of concerning Alfheim can be that it used to be home to the light elves, not the darker ones who inhabited below the earth. Although both races could be classified as Elves but it is the Prose Edda mentions that there is a significant difference between dark and light elves in appearance and the nature.

Light elves are beautiful and beautiful and the majority of people who laid the eyes on them were at ease. The world they lived in is said to be of a pleasing and bright quality. However, Dark elves are vile creatures that lived beneath the earth.

We have no information about either race, other than the descriptions and the nature of the dark and light elves. They were neither prominent in Norse mythology and their worlds are briefly discussed in both the Poetic Edda and the Prose Edda. But, the mention of elves within the Prose Edda might have been inspired by Christian themes, since it suggests that the elves who were light resided in a heaven-like world, which is related to Christian belief systems regarding the heavens and hells.

8. Svartalfheim

Sometimes referred to by the name of Nidavellir, Svartalfheim is the home of the dwarfs. A translation of Svartalfheim is "home to the black elves which is how Vikings as well as Germanic people imagined the race. Nidavellir on the contrary, refers to "low fields," this is related to how Dwarves were believed to reside in underground caverns and caves.

Although it could be confusing for those who read the Eddas as Svartalfheim was described as a dark place where "dark elves" lived but most experts are of the opinion that it was Dwarves who resided there. Furthermore, the darkness of Svartalfheim was not as dark and frightening like Niflheim or Jotunheim it was more of the absence of light. The home of the dwarves is full of caverns underground mines, caverns, and forges, which is why it's normal that the world has only a few lights, unlike Hel which, for instance and was the land of the undead and wicked.

Underground forges and mines in which dwarves resided were the place where they developed strong weapons as well as valuable items. The slim and strong race of dwarves was a skilled craftsmen with a great deal of experience in forging metals and shaping them. As they were skilled they were entrusted by the gods with creating beautiful and valuable objects. The dwarves designed Thor's hammer and Odin's rings and spear. They also created the chain that binds the apocalyptic the wolf Fenrir.

The description of dwarves differs in the lore, with certain sources describing them as "inky black' while others depict their appearance without focusing on their darker skin tone but most believed to the fact that they're a race sensitive to sunlight. Certain sources suggest that dwarves were magical creatures such as the ability to change shape. Despite their size they were also extremely robust, as demonstrated by the formidable weapons they created which none other creature could have made. Another evidence for their power was the fact which Odin assigned four dwarves to carry the skull of Ymir -the sky in Norse mythology - which proves their strength.

9. Helheim

We briefly discussed earlier, Helheim was the underworld where the dead lived. The goddess Hel was the daughter of Loki is the supreme ruler of Hel and was a terrifying character that shattered the hearts of all mortals. Helheim has been believed to lie underground but the exact location along Yggdrasil is not known. We can speculate that it is near the base of the global tree. We've mentioned before that certain sources suggested that people who were sent to Hel were unworthy , while those who were brave were sent to Valhalla. However, this could also be influenced by Christianity and doesn't necessarily represent what Vikings believed before centuries of Snorri's day.

One thing prominently mentioned within Old Norse sources is the route that leads to

Hel which is also often referred to as Helvegr. This particular road is mentioned in the legend of Balder's demise. Balder was considered to be the most loved of gods and most beautiful, and his passing was mourned deeply. The gods tried to revive the Baldur's soul from Hel and consequently they sent an emissary to the underworld to discuss with the queen of Helheim and the goddess Hel.

The emissary was referred to as Hermod, a god of the night. He traveled through the tree of Yggdrasil for nine nights , until the river he came across was known as Gjoll and then he crossed the Gjoll river Gjallarbru and came across a giantess, Modgudr. Modgudr was the protector at the entryway to Helheim however she allowed Hermod into the area, and he continued on his way until he came to an enclosure which was guarded by an enormous dog named Garm.

The stories of Helheim that we have come taken from Snorri Sturluson. Christian beliefs heavily have influenced the stories. Sturluson depicts a gruesome underworld in which the goddess Hel is a slave to its people suffering and misery. Her hall is gloomy and the dead eat at the table of a dining room "hunger," and their knives for eating are considered 'famine. Food is the only way to satisfy their cravings. The beds in the rooms of Hel are called'sick beds' and provide no rest, and ensure that the deceased will have that they have no rest, regardless of how long they rest.

Despite this grim portrayal of Helheim Many experts believe that for the Vikings they believed that the underworld was actually an identical world to the world of the living that the dead participated in activities that were similar from their lives, and, in some cases, even Valhalla where they consumed food, drank, wrestling and even lay down. This is the reason why Vikings were buried with the tools and other items they could use to survive.

Although Helheim is a location in which the dead were in limbo, but not necessarily suffering for ever but there was a significant connection between Helheim and Christian hell. Anyone who ended up in either world was guaranteed to never leave it. Helheim was bound by the Gjoll river. Gjoll that separated Helheim from the other universes according to Norse legends and nobody could get across it once they were was sent to the region. Even Odin did not have the power to release an individual soul from Helheim as demonstrated by Hermod's quest to free Baldur's soul from the grasp of Hel because no one else could do this besides Hermod.

The dead will be permitted to leave the world once Ragnarok begins. Under Loki's guidance the army of dead will be able to march out of Helheim to battle the Aesir as well as Vanir gods, similar to Odin's army, will be fallen warriors that reside inside the halls of Valhalla. The dead will depart

Helheim in a vessel unlike any other, constructed out of the fingernails and toenails from the deceased themselves. Together with Loki is his child Hel Hel, the epitomized queen of underworld.

Chapter 3: The Gods of Norse Mythology

After we've explored the cosmology and myth of the creation of those who belong to the Vikings along with Germanic people It's time to look into the gods themselves. These Norse gods are among the most intriguing creatures of Norse mythology. They were extremely powerful and fascinating personalities, but the most intriguing aspect of these gods was how they shared a lot with human. The gods could have been amazing and awe-inspiring in many ways however, they also had quite some human traits and often had interactions with mortals.

It's an understatement to refer to one of the gods with their most famous name because it could simplify complicated characters and only attribute one attribute to them. Odin is the god of war and magic However, Odin was also the god of wisdom and poetry. He pursued knowledge with such passion that he even lost an eye in pursuit of knowledge and wisdom. A lot of Norse gods were dual in their personality. Some were violent and hateful Some were compassionate and generous, and a lot were both.

In the book, gods were split into two tribes which were called The Aesir as well as the Vanir. They were the Aesir were the principal gods' tribe that had an inherent link to the infinity plane. They were divine Gods, and were gods of the war the shrewd, brave, and duty. They resided within Asgard as well as being associated with order and law throughout the entire universe. Gods from Asgard were guardians who looked over other kingdoms. They guarded them, in particular Midgard from the wrath of other creatures of the universe that could cause chaos if given the chance.

The Vanir On their own were goddesses and gods minor to the world. connected to the earthly plane or natural world. They were gods of harvest, fertility season, the ocean seasons, love, and the sea. Their residence was Vanaheim Many of their followers were peasants as opposed to warriors, who frequently worshipped their Aesir gods of battle and courage.

The primary distinction between the two gods' tribes is the way in which they viewed them. Vikings along with other Germanic people looked at their gods and worshipped them. The Aesir symbolized the social order and justice that were guidelines that govern how a community must be led. This was how the Vikings saw their own society, in which the chieftain was expected to behave similar to the way Odin the king behaved in his kingdom. The Vikings believed in as the

Aesir being more than the gods who ruled courage and war and strength, as evidenced by the reference to Thor's hammer being more than just a weapon capable of devastating destruction. Mjollnir was also employed for social occasions such as marriages and

births, and even deaths.

The Vanir were a people who lived by the laws of nature and the earth. This meant that they did not take part as much in the life of Vikings who were seafaring people who fought wars and raided. The Vanir were more adept at magic than those on Asgard as well as having an alternative view of love as evidenced by their incestuous relationships, in which sisters and brothers were often married. These marriages between siblings and brothers are the ones that include Freyja with her twin brother Freyr and Freyr, who were the children of a union between brother and sister. There are some reports that claim that one of the causes of the Aesir-Vanir conflict was the relationship between siblings which the Aesir hated and thought was dishonorable.

Aesir Gods

Odin

The godfather of the gods and goddesses. Odin is the strongest of all. Odin is the God of Wisdom, poetry, war, and magic. Odin searched for wisdom at every corner and also freely gave it. One of the many facets of Odin's persona was that he was the patron saint of both judges/rulers and outlaws. He was the symbol as a symbol for justice. However, Odin was a trickster who often disguised himself and caused chaos in the realm of mortals which often led to conflicts to erupt to gather warriors for his army at Valhalla.

Despite the way they are depicted of them in pop culture, as exemplary characters and skilled commanders, Odin isn't like the characters is the case in Old Norse myths. Odin did not have a lot of respect for laws and rules and was not a fan for the weak warriors. His blessings were only for those who whom he considered brave that deserved his admiration. Odin was also believed to be to be a god of shamanism, and was a major influence on the shamans. The connection between shamanism and Odin is documented in Old Norse text that mentions the possibility of him traveling through the lands of old while sleeping or dead. To summarize it is hard to conclude that Odin did not care about the motivations for a war or the morality of the action, but more the chaos and destruction.

Odin's rule and power was not limited to the mortals, but also over the gods as well. Odin was the god of Asgard and as the god of Asgard, he was respected and revered. The two gods could be seen in a contrast among Odin as well as Tyr. While Tyr was god of justice and noble battle, Odin was more of god of chaos and magic. This may be the reason why Odin was a fan of many outlaws and gave them his blessings, as did many other figures in the old Germanic mythology and lore.

Odin was a man of two ravens who provided him with news from all across Midgard. Huginn Muninn and Muninn are mentioned within The Poetic Edda as Odin's faithful ravens. This is another indication of the Allfather's connection with Shamanism, since spirit animals and guides accompanied them in many cases. There were also two Wolfs, Geri and Freki, who were committed to gods and were as brave as other animal as part of Norse myths.

Odin was often connected to poetry in Norse mythology. He was acknowledged to communicate effectively and in poetry. It was a gift which he carried, and only gave to those whom he considered worthy. Odin took this mead from the gods of the mythology we'll explore within the next chapter of our book. Since then, the drink is sought after by those looking for wisdom, knowledge and the ability to speak stunning poetry that would be awe-inspiring to the world's mortals. Odin offered the mead to Gods and Goddesses of his choice as well as to a mortal whom Odin served as a patron.

To the Vikings, Odin also had an excellent connection with death. As we've already mentioned Odin was the chieftain in the great hall Valhalla in which the heroic and courageous warriors went when they fell in combat. If it was him or Freyja who was chosen to choose from the first part of souls of the dead or not, it's irrelevant. Whatever the case, for many Vikings or others Germanic people, dying in a dignified manner is the sole way for them to gain entry into Odin's Hall and to live in honour till the close of the time. Following a battle with the help of mythical characters known as 'the Valkyries the Valkyries,' Odin would have his selection of the dead and then they would be admitted to Valhalla.

The Vikings tried to win Odin's approval and favor in battle by killing their adversaries by using a spear, perhaps in honor of the god's weapon, Gungnir in the form of the symbol of power and protection. Offering sacrifices of human beings for Odin were not unusual, but killing someone's sacrifice using the spear was another method of getting to Odin's side. the Vikings.

Being a fervent seeker information and the god of warfare, Odin communicated with the dead. In fact, it is mentioned in the mythology that he could have raised them at times. According to some sources, he spoke to the dead to inquire about their wisdom and knowledge.

Frigg

Frigg is the strongest Aesir goddesses, as well as Odin's wife, which made her as the queen of Asgard. Frigg was the symbol of motherhood to people of the Germanic people, having had mothers like Baldur, Hermod, and Hodor herself. Frigg is also the goddess of marriage and the word Friday taken from her name and that's the reason why Friday was the ideal date to marry in the time of the Vikings. Frigg is often depicted in myths wearing a magnificent blue cape, which symbolizes the sky.

Even though she was wed to the goddess of wisdom Frigg wasn't a simpleton. She was smart and even outwitted Odin at times. The belief is that Frigg was able to predict the future. She was also blessed by the ability of knowing the future, but she didn't make specific predictions regarding the future. This could be the reason why Odin asked her for advice often. As the man she married, Frigg was unfaithful and frequently cheated on Odin. The King and queen of the Aesir frequently bet on the other, and there are many stories of Frigg getting ahead of Odin to achieve the things she wanted.

Despite the various versions that portray Frigg as being unfaithful or devious Frigg was revealed by the Poetic Edda to be a happy wife and mother. The mother wept as her child Baldur was killed and she attempted to save her son however, she was unsuccessful. The prophecy for the future that spoke of Odin's demise was a reference to Frigg's second grief', the loss of her husband during Ragnarok and was a further cause of her discontent. Frigg is believed that she shared many characteristics with goddess Freyja and both were believed to be linked to harvest and fertility in diverse theories of Germanic mythology.

Frigg's home is described as a home in Poetic Edda, and it was known as Fensalir but the precise location of that Frigg's home was not clear. Certain scholars have linked Frigg's world of home with practices that were part of Norse paganism that dealt with swamps and bogs, which suggests that Fensalir could be a place that was brimming with such. But, this could contradict Fensalir's mention within the Prose Edda that described Frigg's world as extremely beautiful.' Frigg was always identified as the equivalent of Odin, and a suitable rival to Odin, the Allfather in terms of intelligence and wisdom.

A significant fact concerning Frigg is that she is among the goddesses who survived Ragnarok. This is a perfect example of one of the most ideal images that many Germanic people used to portray Frigg as the grieving widow and mourning mother.

It's similar to the numerous women of the Viking time who grieved the loss of their loved ones fighting.

Thor

Thor's significance was more than the Viking time. Thor was among the most influential people for the majority of Germanic people prior to the advent of Christianity however, Thor was a unique place in the Vikings who were awed by Thor and believed in the god of thunder as a protector and guardian. Like his father Odin, the King Odin, Thor believed in the law, and was the god people looked to for justice and social stability. Thor is the god of thunder, the sky, as well as, in certain interpretations also, of agriculture.

His mother, Thor's mom was giganticess named Jord The personification of earth. She was also one of Odin's loversand, together they brought Thor into the world. Thor was the protector of not only Midgard but as well Asgard as well, and both worlds depended on the thunder god to protect them. Thor was a formidable warrior and a masculine character with a legend that grew as time passed through generations from one to another. Thor's fame grew due to his achievements in beating giants through a myriad of tales and there are numerous legends of him taking on gigantic beasts for the defense of Asgard as well as Midgard. Other foes he fought bravely against included the serpent of the world Jormungandr.

A noble warrior archetype, Thor was the ideal numerous Vikings wanted to emulate. They admired him and aspired to be as faithful and brave as Thor. Thor was a man with a strong sense of duty that frequently placed him in danger but he never wavered in his fight to protect anyone weak or in need of his assistance. There is a belief that Thor's strength was the strongest in the entirety of Norse mythology. Thor could also become stronger after putting on his megingjord belt. This made him a more formidable warrior. Thor also had a megingjord. But, it earned an honorary place in the mythology of mythological legends immortal - the Hammer of Mjollnir.

Mjollnir is Thor's weapon and he never left home without it. If Thor was thunder, Mjollnir was lightning. Thor was able to channel lightning using the hammer. However, it was also possible to command lightning and thunder without the hammer. The inhabitants of Midgard believed in Thor not only for protection but also for blessing. He blessed weddings , social events by blessing them with Mjollnir and could also be believed to bless objects like land where peasants asked for his blessing prior to when they started planting their crops or constructed structures on land that was undeveloped.

Myths say that Thor traveled through the invisibly and visible planes -as in Midgard and Asgard riding on an chariot that was pulled by two goats Tanngrisnir as well as Tanngnjostr. Thor was able to kill two goats and eat the carcasses before returning them to life using his hammer. they would be as healthy as ever so long they had bones that were still intact. Legend says that the sound of thunder that we hear during the cold and rainy evenings is Thor's chariot firing out of the heavens gates.

In connection with his relationship with floods and rain, Thor was requested to bless the crop and aid people in finding food. The Vikings as well as other Germanic people made sacrifices to the god of thunder to obtain his blessing particularly if sickness and famine became widespread among the population. Thor was even invoked to guard those travelling on ships who would not wish to be victims of storms and torrential rain which could cause danger for ships. Thor had a 3rd magical item , aside from the belt and hammer which were his iron gloves. They were massive and indispensable to utilize Mjollnir.

Thor's importance didn't diminish throughout Scandinavia until the introduction of Christianity. The god of thunder was a formidable character with a fiery temper and the Vikings took inspiration from his example, and often ignoring the rules of other cultures. Yet, Thor was never shown to be clever or deceitful as Loki nor Odin. Thor is straight-forward and is honest and does what he believes is correct, in line with his morality. The inability of him to deceive or be untruthful caused him trouble in the past, since it meant the possibility of falling into a fabled deceit and fraud.

The portrayal of Thor in popular culture isn't true and is vastly different from Norse portrayals. Thor wasn't blonde nor beardless, but he was redheaded and was a man with a thick beard. one of his distinctive features. Another aspect to take into consideration is the temper of Thor. Although he's quick to get angry but he's also demonstrated to be a wise person who is able to think about other options to combat violence. That is to say the man didn't jump into battle, killing massive beasts from left to right when provoked.

Thor's strength and power made him attractive to the Viking warriors However, Thor was also admired by wives who sought him for assistance in overcoming challenges at home, peasants who sought his blessings, and everyone else who needed help. Thor is a God to allpeople, not just warriors. Thor would provide assistance to anyone who needed it even if they were not renowned warriors.

Like many gods Thor is prophesied to die in Ragnarok however, he comes down fighting. Thor is likely to die following his take his revenge on the world serpent Jormungandr. They will fight in a battle that will echo across the universe, however Thor is killed when the serpent poisons his. His sons are spared from the dark ages that the gods have created. Modi Magni and Magni will make use of their father's hammer in order to bring order back in our world. They will bring peace in the new world which rises from the dust of the previous one.

Loki

Despite the representations in popular culture, Loki is not Thor's brother. Loki is the god of tricks of Norse mythology, infamous for insanity and a variety of criminal acts throughout time. Loki is perhaps the most unique god of Germanic mythology, and his status among gods giants, gods, along with other gods is odd. He was he giant, or god? Was he evil or good? Many questions surround Loki and it's difficult to provide definitive answers regarding Loki, the god of tricks.

Loki's father is Jotunn Colorauti in the majority of Old Norse sources. His mother is Laufey may be a giantess or goddess, or something else entirely The sources aren't as plentiful regarding this. In the old stories as Thor and Odin's companion Loki was not concerned about their health or that of any other person mortal or gods, in general. Loki always seemed self-serving as he did whatever he wanted accomplish, regardless of effects and how it might influence the people in his vicinity.

Despite all his mischief, Loki also employed his intelligence and deviousness to aid his gods free of troubles on many occasions. In other instances Loki was the cause of problem. Loki was part of the Aesir tribe however, Loki was also a Jotunn. Loki's gender was a subject of debate in numerous myths. He was typically male however, he was occasionally female. Numerous stories mention the possibility of him changing between genders and other, as In Thrymskvida in The Poetic Edda, which sees the pronouns shifting. The story tells of Thor and Loki's disguise of women in order to recover Thor's stolen hammer from giants.

"Then Loki spake, the son of Laufey:

"As your maid-servant I'll be with ye.

We'll hurry to the home of the giants.'

26. There was a tense waiter, serving-maid,

So, she was able to answer the words of the giant:

"From food, Freyja has spent for eight nights been fasting,

It was so hot that she longed at Jotunheim.'"

Another indication of his androgynous character can be seen in the fact that he was the mother of several of his children, however, he fathered the majority of them, specifically when he concocted the horse Svadilfari to prevent the giant from building his Asgardian wall. Later, he returned with a baby from the horse, and gave birth to Odin's horse and known as the 8-legged Sleipnir. Although he was a keeper of Jotunn blood as well as a bloodline which could trace back to Aesir, Loki is believed to have chosen to gods, rather than giants initially.

Loki is a savage when he can and sometimes with no motive other than amusement, for instance, when he cuts hair of Sif Thor's wife, simply because he thought it was hilarious. Loki often rectified things however, and repaired the issue he caused or damaged, often under duress. For instance, he replaced Sif's cut hair with gold braids that were crafted by the dwarfs made of pure gold. Due to his intelligence, Loki is often called by the Aesir to assist solve issues, even though it's not his fault.

In accordance with his self-serving nature, Loki takes sides based upon what he believes is the best for him and he is able to do so in Ragnarok. Loki will join the side of the giants to fight with them against Aesir as well as in certain Old Norse sources, it is stated that he'll steer his ship of dead (Naglfar) and take them on a journey to battle the gods. It is possible to argue that Loki was forced to fight against the Aesir due to the way they were treated, but then there is also the possible that Loki wasn't a close partner and was never worthy of the harsh treatment he received. The following verse comes directly from Poetic Edda:

"O'er the sea to the north, there's a vessel

Together with the inhabitants of Hel on the helm of the ship is Loki;

The wolf is the first one that wild men follow?

With them Byleist's brother Byleist is also there."

Loki and Heimdall fight during Ragnarok The two are killed by one another. One of the most well-known tales of Loki's nefarious deeds in Norse mythology is the story of how Loki had Baldur killed with deceit, and then carried on with his plan to stop the restitution of Baldur's soul from Hel. Another famous story about Loki is about his connection with Jotunn Angrboda and the Jotunn Angrboda from whom the three monsters he fathered that included The world serpent Jormungand and Queen of the Underworld Hel and the terrifying Wolf Fenrir.

Loki's offspring plays an important part in Ragnarok in which two of them killing Aesir's strongest warriorsFenrir and Jormungand. Fenrir kills Odin and Jormungand kills Thor and kills Thor. It's also possible Loki's offspring, who were the horrific monsters the were forced to their fates. Odin was enraged by Loki's offspring and violently reacted because of his fear. we'll find out what Odin caused in the case of Fenrir and his brothers in the next chapter.

Loki was penalized for his deeds and especially for his role in the demise of Baldur and was to be subject to the same punishment until Ragnarok arrived and Loki was released. Perhaps it was because of his playful nature or because Loki was not an idol, we're not certain, but Vikings as well as other Germanic people didn't worship Loki. Did it be because he represented an exact antithesis of the values that the people of these regions valued : respect as well as loyalty and bravery? It's possible. In any case, there is no evidence of him being or worshipped, and it's possible that Loki was a god of the Vikings hated Loki like the majority of his other Aesir gods did.

Baldur

Baldur is the God of the Aesir recognized for his breathtaking beauty and uncanny wisdom. Baldur resolved disputes between rival mortals and gods and settled disputes in a calm, wise manner by using his charisma and humor. There are some versions that say that Baldur was so physical fair and attractive that light was able to shine from his body. This is why it's not a surprise that Baldur's demise was one of the most significant incidents in Norse mythology. It was a tragic event that everyone mourned Gods and mortals alike.

Baldur was the most beautiful ship ever constructed: Hringhorni. Baldur also rode the horse Lettfeti. He lived in a beautiful palace known as Breidablik that was so stunning that Odin was awestruck by its splendor. The Allfather was a visitor to Baldur's palace and wrote about the palace as in The Poetic Edda as:

"The seventh one is Breithablik; Baldr has there

To him, a house set

In the land, I am aware that it is so fair

From the evil, fate is free."

Baldur had some Brothers from his dad Odin as well as many half-brothers which included Thor himself. He married the goddess Nanna as well as their child Forseti was a great example the wisdom of their father as well as admiration for justice. Forseti was able to settle disputes just as did Baldur and was believed as a symbol of justice and peace. Baldur's story is among the most popular stories of Norse mythology. We'll look into it in the next section. Beyond this, there's not much information about him aside from his status as a appreciated and admired by the Vikings as well as others Germanic people.

Heimdall

We briefly talked about Heimdall before who is the protector for his Aesir world of

Asgard. He protects it from Himinbjorg and his home on or above the Bifrost, always vigilant and watchful. Heimdall is a sleeper and is much less sleep-deprived than mortals and gods. The hearing he had was that impressive, he could hear the grass growing as well as wool being sown on sheep. He also could see miles of distance and be able to see the same way at night as in the early morning.

From his position where Heimdall monitors for intruders and if he sees any, he'll blast his grand Horn Gjallarhorn that can be heard throughout heaven and in the underworld. He'll sound the horn during the time of Ragnarok when enemies appear towards the surface. Heimdall was Odin's son. He is a figure who is highly revered by Vikings as well as the other Germanic people. Some sources declare him to be the father of humanity due to the fact that the mortals he taught him many things that are mentioned in various Old Norse sources.

There is a belief that the concept of classes in society was created for the benefit of humanity by Heimdall. He was believed to have wandered around Midgard in disguise, offering tips to the people around him, particularly couples.

According to some sources, Heimdall was the son of nine sisters, maidens, that was an attainable feat for gods, however, not mortals. He explains this in the poem Heimdalargaldr where the poet writes: Of 9 mothers, am I the son and of nine sisters am I the son of nine sisters. He was armed with the massive sword known as the "head," and older sources suggested that he was gifted with the ability of foresight and could see at the future.

Tyr

Tyr is among the gods that have been around for centuries in Germanic mythology and, despite being linked with war, there's plenty of information we don't know about this god. Tyr was not only a god of war, but also peace as he was associated with justice and treaties. He didn't want or encourage war like Odin did and was a part of the battle. to every aspect of the war, including its conclusion.

Even though Tyr's significance diminished during the Viking times prior to Christianity and long before Tyr was a major god of the early Germanic people. The god was also popular in Roman culture, however the Romans also named him Mars as the god of war, too. This is evident in the linguistic linkage with the date 'Tuesday' and is associated with Mars and Tyr. Tyr as well as Mars.

Tyr was responsible for ensuring the law and order and spreading justice. He was also brave as was evident in the story about the binding of Fenrir which is the most significant mythology we have about Tyr. In this tale, Tyr offered his arms to ensure Fenrir was bound and wouldn't cause harm to anyone. The sacrifice of Tyr is often compared to that of Odin sacrifice of his eye to learn more.

Vanir Gods

Freyja

Freyja is most likely the most famous goddess in the Vanir tribe, who resided on Vanaheim initially, prior to being transferred to Asgard following the war and thus living amid the Aesir. Although we know for certain that her father's name is Njord but we do not know her mother's name. She had a brother named Freyr and they were married in the past in time, just as many of the siblings and brothers from that tribe Vanir tribe were prior to the war.

Freyja is frequently linked to love and fertility, lust, and beauty. There is a legend that says her beauty was exceptional and everyone who met her admired her. Freyja is said to be a cry of gold tears and could transform into a falcon whenever she wanted in particular when she visited Hel.

Freyja loved these qualities that were given to her and she was a lover of beauty love, sexuality, and love. She was sexually wild in a manner, and it's claimed that she slept with numerous males. Loki even accused her of sleeping with all people and elves. This could have been true. In the end, Freyja liked to indulge in passion and pleasure.

But, Freyja was much more than a beautiful face. She was an adept practitioner of magic. In certain sources she was also described as the goddess of battle and war. As we have mentioned before, Freyja is believed to have to have half the souls the fallen warriors who died in the war for her realm, Folkvangr.

Freyja was closely connected to specific forms of Old Norse magic and shamanism specifically, Seidr. The practitioners of this kind of magic weren't always trying to fight an entity as powerful as the Norns however, they operated within the bounds of fate and attempted to create positive changes. Freyja was regarded as a goddess of the gods, possessing supernatural and shamanic powers that included being able to change into the falcon.

Freyr

Freyr was a god of fertility in Germanic mythology. He's been associated with the sun and the abundance. Freyr was among the most popular gods in his fellow members of the Vanir tribe of goddesses and gods. His standing as god of fertility and harvest made him an important position for Scandinavian people prior to the Viking period - they were primarily farmers, and needed an idol like Freyr to aid them. A few sources mention the existence of a cult around Freyr that goes to demonstrate his importance to the Germanic farmers from Scandinavia.

Even though the family was prominent that included Njord as father, as well as Freyja as his mother, evidence suggests the fact that Freyr was more revered than Njord was. Many historical locations are associated with Freyr, the Vanir God Freyr and pre-Viking stories from Scandinavia mention rituals and prayers dedicated to Freyr, the goddess of fertility. Some believe Freyr's real name was Yngvi-Freyr. This could mean that he was one of the paternal ancestors to the Swedish royalty of King of Sweden.

In spite of the old stories about his first marriage to Freyr, his younger sister Freyr was believed to be later married to Jotunn Gerdr. She was also considered to have been a deity. They had a son named Fjolnir. Freyr's mate is a huge boar, named Gullinbursti and Freyr rode to the funeral of Baldur. Although Freyr was frequently linked to fertility as well as agricultural however, Freyr was also a courageous warrior with combat expertise. Freyr even fights bravely against the giant of fire Surtr during Ragnarok and then dies fighting.

However, the main purpose of Freyr for the Vikings as well as the Germanic people prior to them was to be the god of fertility to whom they offered prayers for the harvest to be successful. He could control sunlight and rain, and people prayed for his blessing so that they will succeed. Agriculture was associated with prosperity in the past and those who had good yields prospered. Freyr was also associated with the virtues of virility, and was often invoked at weddings and other social occasions because Freyr was believed to bring peace and joy at will. Freyr was often offered sacrifices particularly during harvest festivals and the animal sacrificed was typically boar.

Freyr was adored and adored by mortals, but also by gods. The Aesir was taken as a hostage towards the conclusion of the Aesir-Vanir war. He quickly became one of them and was not hated by any. Gods too required sexual power and abundant wealth in wealth and harvest So Freyr's spot among them was revered and admired. Freyr was the ruler of Alfheim which might mean that he was the ruler of the elves who were light in appearance, but it's not clear. Old Norse sources don't mention the light elves, so it could be a speculation at the best. He was the captain of the ship Skidbladnir and was assisted by the wind.

Njord

Njord is the godfather of Freyja as well as Freyr. Njord was known as the Vanir god of fishing, hunting as well as sea-faring and wind, and was associated with prosperity and fertility like many Vanir Gods. An ancient Scandinavian quote reveals the god's relationship to wealth, which is 'as wealthy as Njord. Njord was transported to Asgard together with Freyja and Freya and is an honourary participant in the Aesir gods' tribe and Freya as well. The place of Njord's residence in Asgard is called Noatun, which means'ship enclosure' and he was connected with the sea once more to the point that he lived his life by the sea.

The most important story in Norse mythology that mentions Njord is his wedding with the giantess Skadi who had traveled to Asgard to seek revenge for the death of her father. The gods offered Skadi the option of choosing one of the gods she wanted to marry, so that there would be peace. She chose Njord in a flurry of coincidence believing that it was Baldur. The couple's marriage didn't last many years and was miserable. Skadi was not a fan of Njord's life at the beach and he was averse to the cold mountains where she stayed. They couldn't adjust to one another's temperament The marriage was brief and ended abruptly.

Njord was believed to be an significant to those living in Scandinavia and some places are named in his honor even to this day such as Naerum (translation"Njord's home")) located in Denmark.

Chapter 4: Myths, Legends, and Creatures

This chapter will go over some of the more well-known stories and legends of Norse mythology, handed through the centuries. We'll learn the story of how Thor's hammer was taken and how he was able to get it returned. We'll explore the story of Loki's imprisoning and how it led to an unlucky incident which set off the twilight for the gods as well as the completion of time. The most fascinating aspect of the myths of Norse folklore is that each one highlights specific characteristics of the gods, characters, as well as creatures that are the focus of the story. But, more importantly the stories may reflect the characteristics associated with those who were Germanic people and the way they saw the world, and sought to understand it through their devotion to Gods larger than life.

The Aesir-Vanir War

In the wake of the last chapter, let's discuss the war between Aesir and Vanir that has been briefly mentioned in the past. There aren't many books detailing the details of this battle However, it was discussed in the two Eddas and the Bible, and we can get an idea of the way it began. It is believed that peace was maintained between the two gods' tribes initially and they lived with harmony. Sometimes, they met to play games or engage in lively debate. It is also probable that Aesir were averse to or feared towards their fellow Vanir for their way of life that did not adhere to any rules or boundaries and was evident by their sexually sexy relationships.

One day , everything changed. A Vanir goddess named Gullveig was a visitor to the gods of Aesir in their hall of greatness in Asgard She rambled over her love for things that are materialistic, including gold. This upset the Aesir gods, who hated remarks about minor things. They determined that Gullveig was to be executed for her recklessness and they would do this world an favor in getting rid it of a smug person such as this. In the end, she was shot to death with a variety of spears, and then thrown her corpse into burning fires that surrounded Odin's hall. However, something was off.

Gullveig emerged from the flame unharmed. The Aesir gods, as stunned at first, did it again. They killed her and fed her corpse to the flames for two times more and, each time, the flame would expel Gullveig out without injury. Gullveig proved to be a formidable sleuth and a practitioner for dark spells. The task of killing her was as easy. It was believed that the Vanir gods as well as goddesses were extremely annoyed by the way the Aesir took a pity on as one of them which is why they took to the streets to scream revenge and plans for war were started. All-seeing Odin was aware of Vanir's plans for Vanaheim and the Aesir also began preparing for war against Asgard.

The conflict was bloody and bloody Odin's spear pounded the first blow to all of the Vanir ranks. Despite the power of the Aesir and the Vanir, the Vanir were not easy prey. They employed their skills in magic to gain an advantage, and destroyed all Asgardian walls. The Aesir moved on Vanaheim and did the same destruction. The longer the two gods' tribes were at war, the clearer was that there would be no winner to emerge from the battle and that both Aesir along with the Vanir were going to suffer huge losses. The battle was more a result of exhaustion the conflict than wisdom of the gods that led them to gather for a possible peace treaty and to stop the war.

The tribes debated for hours over the true motive for the conflict and who was responsible. To prevent a return to death and bloodshed Gods and gods decided to a truce and agreed to restore things to how they were before when the two tribes were peacefully living together. The tribes were united and, to ensure that there was no chance of a breach of the agreement and exchange hostages, both parties agreed to exchange hostages. The chiefs of the Vanir tribe included Njord and his sons, Freyja and Freyr, and they travelled with open arms to Asgard. They were from there, the Aesir, Mimir and Hoenir (which could be a different term for the earliest gods Odin's son Vili) were taken to Vanaheim.

Mimir was considered to be one of the gods with the most wisdom and was a huge source of wisdom, serving as an advisor for gods. However Mimir was also a god of the

Vanir. Vanir believed that the Aesir was a swindler and had deceived them. The Vanir had elected Hoenir as their ruler , with the skilled Mimir with him However, Hoenir seemed incapable of taking a decision without Mimir and this led to the Vanir to suspect a plot. The Vanir cut off the head of Mimir to pay homage and then handed it over to Odin who wished to protect the wisdom inside his head. So he blessed the head that was cut off with magical herbs and cast an spell to ensure Mimir was able to survive.

In spite of the incident, harmony between Aesir and Vanir was not shattered. They met again to stop a conflict from erupting, as well as to agree that the execution of Mimir would not affect the peace. They signed the new peace agreement in the same way they normally did it by throwing into a cauldron. The two gods coexisted harmoniously as they will remain for a long time until Ragnarok. They also added value to their lives by Freyja as an example giving lessons to Odin Seidr which was a powerful magical device that enabled Odin to look into the future and perform many other feats. Seidr was believed to be an effective magician, something Odin was not averse to However, many other men did not.

There are a variety of variations and variants of the story each one interesting and some of them even make sense. Certain experts think that Gullveig was in reality the real Freyja herself disguised. Freyja had been known to travel between towns disguised, attempting Seidr and sometimes working even for hire. When she entered the temple of the Aesir gods They were initially fascinated by her powerful powers. The gods of order, law, and wisdom soon realized that they were wrong however, and recognized that they couldn't abandon the ideals of order and honor to gain quick results from magic. Their blame was Freyja for enthralling them with her power and revealing to the Aesir part of them that they didn't like. Then, they slashed Freyja and threw her into flames.

It is also believed that a creature came into existence from the spit of Aesir as well as the Vanir gods, in the second Peace Treaty Kvasir. He was the most intelligent human to ever stroll through Midgard and was aware of everything that needed to be learned. There was not a single question could not be answered by him. He traveled the globe dispersing his wisdom to everyone who were seeking it. One day, everything was stopped, Kvasir was killed and his wisdom could no longer be transferred to others. But the mead of poetics was made by the blood of his deceased father.

Odin and the Mead of Poetry

The poem is discussed in depth throughout the Prose Edda, though there could be slight differences in Old Norse poems that preceded Snorri Sturluson. The gods of Aesir and Vanir chose not to let their words be wasted, which is why they made Kvasir from it, in the wake of the second peace agreement. Kvasir's knowledge about the worlds in nine was unsurpassed and he made use of it to address questions of people.

Kvasir's journeys led Kvasir to the home of two dwarfs named Galar And Fjalar. They made up stories to Kvasir and claimed they had an issue important enough and required counselling, and they took him to a place where they could talk an intimate conversation. The dwarfs killed Kvasir and drained the blood of him into a cauldron as well as two huge containers. The cauldron was named Odrerir and the jars, or jugs were called Bodn and Son. Fjalar as well as Galar included honey in the blood of Kvasir. This created an unique mead that would allow any drinker to become a poet , or an intelligent man.

The Aesir gods were anxious when Kvasir was not back, and they sent a messenger to inquire about Kvasir. Fjalar and Galar explained to them that Kvasir was dead in a coma, choked on his own brains because no one could ever ask him a sharp enough question. The dwarves were a bit rash in inviting a giant named Gilling to dinner. Gilling as well as his spouse after killing Kvasir. Fjalar Galar and Fjalar Galar carried Gilling out to ocean on a vessel, while they were rowing the boat, they turned it upside down. Gilling was unable to swim, and drowned. the two dwarves just placed the boat on its side and then rowed it back to home.

Gilling's wife found out about her husband's passing her heart broke she cried in pain and mourned his loss. The dwarves asked her if Gilling would find some peace in gazing at the ocean towards the direction where Gilling was drowned. She replied yes. Galar got up over the door she stood at and threw a massive stone over her head the widow being killed and suffocating her crying. The son of the giants Suttung was furious after learning about the demise of his parents following the search for them out after they refused to return to their home. Suttung was determined to find the dwarfs to exact revenge.

Suttung caught the two dwarves who were a danger to themselves and, along with them, headed for the middle of the ocean. There he laid Fjalar as well as Galar on a tiny rock that was just a little above the waves, and set to sink in the near future. The dwarves were aware that the sea could quickly drown them and the shoreline was too far away for them to swim to it. Out of options and desperate The dwarves pleaded with Suttung to show mercy and offered him the poem as a compensation for the loss. Suttung brought the two jars along with the cauldron to his mountain home, Hnitbjorg. He stored the liquid in the mountain's heart and appointed his daughter Gunnlod to act as an attentive guardian for this precious cauldron.

It wasn't long before word to spread to the Aesir about the death of Kvasir as well as the mead of poetry and Odin was determined to recover the mead to himself. The man disguised as Odin was dubbed Bolverkr which translates to grieving worker, and traveled to Jotunheim. On one occasion, Bolverkr found nine men working in a field. However, their efforts were ineffective and their progress was sporadic because they were using dull scythes which could barely cut grass. Odin met with the men and discovered they worked for Suttung's sister, Baugi, and a plan was devised.

Odin offered the workers to sharpen their scythes and they gladly accepted Odin's suggestion. The scythes that were sharpened were extremely sharp, and the farmers were able to cut fields more quickly.

They wanted to purchase Odin's whetstone in order to make their scythes sharper at will. Odin refused to let them buy the item, however. He tossed it in the air, and as he scrambled to find it, the workers attacked each other's throats and instantly died. Odin picked up his whetstone and continued his journey. At night of the day, he came across Baugi's farm.

The giant was a bit upset as he lost nine workers at this point in the season. This meant that he would be unable to find them which would mean his harvest would be affected. This is the time Odin offered to take on the work of nine workers for a drink from his mead of poems Baugi's brother owned. Although Baugi was in need of assistance, he wasn't able to accept the request since his brother already had the mead. He finally agreed to travel together with Odin up to Suttung's mountain in order to request his brother an alcoholic drink from poetry mead.

In disguise in disguise as Bolverkr, Odin continued to work throughout the summer. He did the same work that nine men typically perform. The season came to an end, Odin went to Baugi to claim his prize. The giant was with Odin and they travelled to the Suttung's house. Baugi informed his brother of the agreement he struck with Bolverkr and asked that the man be allowed drinking privileges from mystic mead. Suttung refused to entertain their request in any way and was determined to not let one drop of the mead go away from the mountain.

Odin suggested to Baugi that they'd have manipulate Suttung to gain access to the mead of poetry and Baugi accepted. Odin made an auger or drill known as Rati and then directed Baugi to create into the mountain Hnitbjorg in which the mead was hidden inside an underground chamber. This giant was at work for a long time and then told Odin that he was done. The moment Odin was able to blow into the hole that Baugi made, stone chips hit his face, which meant that Baugi was lying when he claimed that he was done. Odin directed Baugi to keep drilling until he could make an incision through the mountain. When Baugi declared he was finished and Odin blows air and the chips were blown through the mountain. They were successful.

Odin transformed into a serpent in a flash and scared Baugi, who attempted to stab Odin with an auger, however, Odin had already passed through the gap. Odin assumed the form of Bolverkr when he was in the secret chamber where the mead was kept. Gunnlod sat in the chamber watching the liquid but she was unable to maintain her precautity when she gazed at Bolverkr. Bolverkr enticed her and stayed for the night with her for three glasses of the mead. At the end of period of three weeks,

Gunnlod was unable to deny any request that he was given.

At the beginning of his drink Odin took the cauldron and emptied it of Odrerir the second Son along with the 3rd Bodn. After taking in the entire poem, Odin changed himself into an eagle before flying off to Asgard. Suttung noticed Odin flying off from his sky. He then saw that the gigantic transformed into an eagle and it was chase time. The eagles flew over Jotunheim and walked towards Asgard which is where they met with the rest of Aesir gods spotted what was happening and made containers to keep the mead of poetry.

In a rush, Odin spat the mead into the vessels that were prepared for him. However, during his hurry, some spilled out from his back. It was never kept, so anyone could claim the mead. According to legend, the mead which came from Odin's back was the one that was gifted to poets who were not as talented and is the reason they were inspired. The remainder of the mead that the Aesir gods kept for their own as well, and Odin could occasionally give it to his deemed worthy poets.

Another aspect of the tale that was reported in a few sources was the fact that the Aesir were ready to create massive fires within the wall of Asgard when they saw Suttung following the Allfather. After Odin was within these walls they ignited these flames and let the flames inflict pain on Suttung's wings and he fell into the flames of ablaze and died.

Odin's Sacrifice

As we said earlier, Odin was a relentless seeker of wisdom and knowledge and was willing to pay the highest price for both. One instance of his desire to know is the effort to understand and discover the runes from Yggdrasil. Runes were essentially letters that were used by the Vikings as well as other Germanic people communicated with before switching back to Latin alphabet a few centuries later. However, they had greater symbolic value than the ability to communicate words. They were an uncanny force that could hold the key to unlocking the mysteries of the universe. And anyone who could comprehend them could transform the world. That's why Odin's mission to decipher these runes wasn't only to comprehend a few sentences or even words. This was an effort to connect to an incredibly mysterious source.

We discussed earlier the Norns who are among the most fearsome beings in the entire Norse mythology. They had power over the fate of men, and they debated and conducted judgment from their home at foundation of Yggdrasil. One of the ways that fates determined men's destiny was through carving runes onto the trunk of The world tree. Since Yggdrasil connects all the planets in the universe the runes carved upon its trunk could convey the Norns their will across all the worlds and causing change all over the world starting from Asgard all the way to Hell and everywhere between them.

From his perch at the top of Asgard, Odin envied the Norns for their power and ability to influence destiny. He longed for that wisdom and knowledge, and was prepared to go to any lengths to acquire the Norns' wisdom. The runes were discovered within the water of Urd (Urdarbrunnr) Urdarbrunnr, the source of the water that feeds Yggdrasil and also the Norns residence at the foot of the tree. Odin traversed the tree's trunk Yggdrasil towards Urd to find out about the mysteries of runes. But the secrets would only be made available only to those who were worthy of gaining the power of Odin.

So, Odin hung himself from the branches of Yggdrasil for nine days and nine nights. He killed himself using his strong knife Gungnir and gazed upon the darkness that flowed from Urd and the tree's trunk in anticipation of the runes to come out. Numerous gods visited the place the hanger was hung and offered assistance however Odin directed them to not help him and let the man hang without so much as a sip of water.

Odin's journey was tough and he was barely able to endure the long nine days without the lack of food or water from the Yggdrasil. The sacrifice he made was effective at the end of the ninth day when runes were revealed. The runes showed more than shapes or symbols but were also able to reveal their secret and wisdom they contain. Odin was able to end his crucible, and climbed off the tree. He told his story as follows:

"Then I got fertilized, and was able to discern the truth;

I truly thrived and grew.

From one word to another I was then led to the word "word"

From a project to the job, I felt able to be led to a job."

Odin's understanding of the runes was vast, and it led him to become an extremely powerful gods across the entire universe. Odin was blessed with ability to heal and defeat his foes easily which rendered their weapons useless against his power. He was able to communicate with dead and raise them and could perform whatever great thing his mind could think of.

Odin's sacrifice can be seen by the account of the moment he lost his vision. The sacrifice was also part of the never-ending quest to gain knowledge or wisdom. Odin was aware of the well at Mimir and its significance as the wisdom of all. He set out to gain the wisdom of Mimir, and was willing to pay whatever price it took to acquire this valuable information. When Odin reached the well, he met Mimir who was the protector for the water. The well's every drop held wisdom and knowledge and the well's guardian would never take one drop of water lightly.

Mimir informed Odin in the course of their conversation that Allfather was required to sacrifice an eye to drink a glass of water from the well. We don't have any method of determining how that exchange went however we do are certain that Odin accepted the heavy cost, and sacrificed his eye in order to take drinking water from the well. He cut his eye and dropped it into the well. After the money was settled, Mimir took his horn out and threw into the well and gave Odin his promised water drink. After drinking his beverage, Odin was blessed with an inexhaustible amount of wisdom and knowledge.

Thor's Hammer and the Giant

Thor's Hammer Mjollnir was his favorite and he would always sleep on it with his back. In the morning, Thor got up and stretched. He pulled out his hammer, and was enraged.

Mjollnir was nowhere to be seen. Thor was looking everywhere for his hammer since in the absence of it, realms of gods and humans alike could be in peril. Thor required it to safeguard Asgard and Midgard as well as Midgard, and without it, everyone would be at risk against the attack of the giants of frost.

Thor was able to ask his wife Sif whether she had ever been to Mjollnir or had any idea where it was however, she had no details. Thor's daughters, along with his, assisted in the search and in the process, they transformed his house upside-down.

Mjollnir was not to be located. Thor was shocked to realize that it must have been Loki who took it, as Loki was a fool, and it was something he'd perform just for the enjoyment of it. Thor discovers Loki however, Loki, the god of mischief, insists that it wasn't he who took it, and it wouldn't be similar to that.

Loki however, had an idea. Thor sought Freyja for help and she was willing to help. She provided Loki and Loki her falcon-like dress that allowed the wearer to develop wings like birds and fly. Loki altered his appearance and travelled to Jotunheim the realm of the giants. He believed that they stole the hammer. Loki returned to his former form after arriving and requested an appointment with the leader of the giants Thrym who confessed to having stolen Thor's Hammer. He claimed it was hidden deep in the ground 8 miles below the surface. He declared that the hammer would not be returned until the Aesir offered the hand of Freyja's bride.

Devastated by the news, Loki returned to Asgard and announced the news. The gods were angry especially Freyja who was upset by the idea to marry an enormous pay the ransom for Thor's hammer. The council that Heimdall was in suggested that Thor goes through Jotunheim in disguise in the form of Freyja herself. In Jotunheim, he could recover his hammer, and then inflict a horrendous vengeance on the giant who took the hammer. Thor did not approve of the idea. Thor was a courageous and noble warrior who had no deceit in his character and this kind of trickery was not something he would have approved of. He also believed that all gods would be mocked should he accept this unmanly plan. Yet, Loki convinced him that this was the only method to get his hammer. If Thor did not agree, Asgard might soon succumb to the control of the giants. As a man who prioritized duty above everything else, as he usually does, Thor agreed.

Thor was dressed in an elegant wedding dress and donned precious stones and jewels to disguise his identity as Freyja. He summoned his chariot to be pulled by goats and, together with Loki dressed as his servant, they journeyed to Jotunheim to rescue Mjollnir. The gigantic Thrym was thrilled to be able to see Freya arriving and instructed his men to prepare the venue for a celebration that would be worthy of the most beautiful of all goddesses. Thrym boasts that, when he had Freyja being his wife, he was blessed with the most precious possessions a giant could want.

Thrym hired his servants to escort Thor and Loki disguised as maidens, to the mansion, and give them the warm welcome from the giants. The chieftain of the giants threw an extravagant banquet that was worthy of Freyja in which Thor could have revealed his the real face of his. Thor ate eight salmon as well as an entire ox as well as three mead barrels in addition to the cake for weddings. Thrym was initially impressed however he soon began to doubt the more Thor consumed. He told him he'd not seen an individual woman eat like Freyja. This is when Loki's cleverness and wit were important, and he asserted that Freyja was so excited and in love to see Thrym that she'd not had a meal for the last week.

In awe of the response, Thrym nodded and was instantly overwhelmed by a powerful wish to hug Freyja. He came closer and lifted the veil that covered Thor's face only to be greeted by intense red eyes staring at Thor. Thor not able to contain his rage. Thrym was stunned and shocked. He claimed he'd never before had an emaciated bride before with such eyes. Loki was back and asserted that Freyja was also unrestful in anticipation of meeting the huge Lord.

Thrym requested Mjollnir to be carried to the wedding in order to bless it according to tradition and then to be presented to Freyja to make her wedding perfect. That was the moment Thor became excited, as the moment was near for him to be brought back together with his Hammer. After the hammer had been placed before his face, Thor snatched Mjollnir by the handle and killed Thrym and his companions, which included his entire family. Thor along with Loki went back to Asgard as a triumphant pair, and with Mjollnir secured in the hands of its owner.

Chapter 5: Norse Paganism

The Old Norse Religion

The Christian faith we are familiar with is in its peak during the time of the fall of Rome in 476 CE until the beginning of the Viking Age in 793 CE. Although this Viking Age is extremely celebrated but it is crucial to keep in mind that many countries were already converted or started to switch to Christianity at that point. Denmark officially converted to Christianity around 990 CE at the time of the close of the Viking Age. The other Scandinavian nations were converted a century later and in the year 1000 CE and Sweden being the first to convert in the 1066 CE and also marking the conclusion of the Viking Age. In Sweden however, Christianity wasn't properly established until around the middle of the 12th century.

It may seem odd to think that the time period that most people think of as to be the height of the Old Norse religion, was actually when the religion started to decline, and then declined. The time that was the time of Vikings was a period of significant changes in religion throughout The Scandinavian Peninsula and Iceland. The majority of modern scholars discredit the myth of the antichrist-hating Vikings. Although the majority of Scandinavian population was actually pagan at the time that it was the Viking Age began, many Vikings simply added the Christian god to their pantheon of own gods. The numerous attacks on churches and monasteries had less to do with religion, and more related to the wealth they could accumulate in their possessions. There was a very low risk when it came to raiding monasteries. While they were a straightforward attack, they were also very attractive.

It is possible that this is why the Viking Era is highly celebrated because , when the Norse people left Scandinavia and settled in Northwestern Europe, it helped spread the Norse faith, just as Christian missionaries were able to do with Christianity. The mass emigration to search of agricultural land included areas such as Iceland as well as the Shetland Islands and The Faroe Islands, and the Orkneys. The entire region was extremely sparsely populated, and they were easily absorbed into Norse tradition and religion.

In the last 800 years CE In the late 800s CE, the settlers from Norway settled in Iceland and introduced Iceland's Old Norse faith. Toponymy implies that In Iceland, Thorr was the most popular god, whereas Odinn does not appear to have been present in the island. Freyr was also a popular god in Iceland. The 'Hrafnkels Saga' also mentions the existence of a priest from Freyr. Other areas that are densely populated where Vikings were able to migrate to, including England, Scotland, Southwest Wales as well as southwest Wales and the Western Isles, Ireland, and the Isle of Man, bear evidence of the Norse religion and culture. A large portion of this is toponymy, but there's evidence from archeological excavations to prove the spreading that of Old Norse religion.

In reality, it was Viking attacks that brought Norse into contact with Christianity. After they settled in areas with a large Christian population, such as Ireland and Normandy They converted to Christianity rapidly. There aren't many modern sources that prove this, but it's evident from archeological evidence. Since the Norse were buried in customary fashion with grave goods while Christians were not, the change in the religion of their time is simple to recognize. Apart from the being converted out from those areas of Scandinavian Peninsula and Iceland, there were German as well as Anglo-Saxon missionaries that visited Norse villages to help convert the Norse to convert them.

The thing that hindered keeping information about information on Old Norse religion was that Christians assumed control of what were until then traditional pagan sites. For instance In Uppsala, Sweden, the remains of a former church were discovered alongside the massive Norse burial mounds.

Because that the Old Norse religion was mainly oral, the majority of the writings that exist on it are from Tacitus one of the most influential Roman historians. Tacitus was a historian whose writings contributed to the understanding of the later Old Norse religion, was also the writer of the Germania.' "Germania" was written in the year the year 98 CE and was initially titled "On the Origin and Situation of the Germans." It's an ethnographic, historical document that outlines the customs, laws, and lands of the Germanic people who were not part of the Roman Empire, comprising those who were the closest to Roman areas and the ones who lived near the coastlines of the Baltic. Together with Scandinavian artifacts archaeologists have discovered, this is our principal source of information regarding the religion and practices that characterized the Scandinavian people.

As per Tacitus, Germanic people had priests who preferred open-air locations to be their holy places and were adamant about the art of fortune-telling, augury and even sacrifice. The rituals was incorporated in all aspects of Norse living of people. Their faith was crucial in the context of warfare and social life as well as daily life. It's been classified as an "non-doctrinal community religion" and an ethnic religion. It differs in structure and practice among different peoples and regions in part due to cultural or social differences, but as a result of the influence of word-of-mouth.

History of Norse Paganism

To comprehend Norse Paganism, one must first understand its roots, which lie deep within the history. Early evidence for people arriving in Scandinavia dates back around 10,000 BCE. Most people are influenced by

Vikings when they think of their Old Norse religion. In reality, the Viking Era was just a small part of Old Norse Paganism.

The first people to settle in the Scandinavian Peninsula were the Sami people, whose ancestry is still a subject of debate by Anthropologists. Germanic people migrated North in the late 1700s There is a lack of evidence of what went in the region between the bronze and copper periods. We are aware that the inhabitants there practiced a type which was part Germanic Paganism, which is the principal branch of the which Old Norse paganism is split. The roots of the original Germanic religion are prehistorical which, in turn is what makes them difficult to discover. The majority of information we have regarding our understanding of the Old Norse religion comes from the writings from the early Christian Missionaries Latin writer, or archeological discoveries like amulets, cultic artifacts and grave items.

As per Anders Andren, a professor of archaeology at Stockholm, Sweden, the Old Norse religion is a "cultural patchwork." Anthropologists believe that Germanic Paganism was the original religion of the Indo-European people. Numerous faith systems and religions stemmed from Proto-Indo-European mythology. They later split and developing into distinct branches, such as Anglo-Saxon Paganism and the Norse system. The religion was mostly passed down through oral or codified texts. It was so deeply rooted in oral traditions that Old Norse religion ended up not being stable nor uniform. However it was true that the Norse most likely believed they were an equal entity despite the differences in their practices, since they shared a common language, which was the Old Norse.

Although the word Old Norse religion first appeared in around 200 BCE, during the Proto-Norse time period, practitioners could be further back. In that period the Norse people separated from the primary Germanic pagan branch and became an independent group of Germanic people. In the end, it was a Germanic system. Germanic system is very like the Germanic system, in that they revered Wodan and gods like the Norse with very minor distinctions. 200 BCE is the date in which historians established there existed a significant distinction between the Norse pagans who lived in Scandinavia as well as Germanic Pagans in Germany.

The first time any rituals were practiced in Scandinavia was around the year 500 BCE that was the beginning in the Iron Age. Norse religions date back to 10000 BCE however. The absence of evidence from the period is likely because copper and bronze are not as durable as iron, so it's logical to discover more archeological sites that date back to earlier in the Iron Age. Also, 500 BCE is a lot closer to when we first discovered evidence for human beings living in

Scandinavia many thousands many years earlier. It's difficult to accept the possibility that we do not have any way to know 10 000 years of Norse religions. The pace of development for society wasn't as rapid at the time as it is today. It was at the beginning of the modern age and we can conclude that they essentially worshipped the same gods, but with different names. It is also believed it is believed that they believed in the Old Norse religion originated there in the way we know it today.

Post-Christian Era

The Norse were not a nation with a word for "religion.. Prior to the advent of Christianity The Old Norse religion was regarded by Heathens more as a way of living rather than a religious belief. It's almost comical that the desire to categorize religions based on the Old Norse ways of life and their worship as a religion was precisely because its practitioners were seeking to be distinguished and differentiated from

Christians. The term"old custom" was first used in the post-Christian age which classified the belief system that was practiced by the Norse as an individual religion. After the advent of Christianity and the advent of Christianity, it was at this point that the Norse began to differentiate the Norse into "old custom" (Forn sid) that was a reference to practices that were practiced during the pre-Christian age and "heathen custom" (heidinn sid) that was a reference to practices that placed the emphasis on rituals, actions and behaviors, not beliefs and belief.

The religion involved the worship of a variety of gods, goddesses as well as other gods. The gods were split into two distinct groups, referred to in the AEsir as well as the Vanir which included Odinn as well as Thorr being among the most famous characters. The Norse gods also form included in the Eddas. They are also part of the Eddas. Eddas include the two Medieval

Icelandic works, the "Poetic Edda" and the 'Prose Edwardda.. It is believed that the "Poetic Edda" is composed of unpublished poems, whereas"the "Prose Edda" (also known as the "Younger Edda") was composed by an Icelandic poet and politician, Snorri Sturluson. It is not clear if Sturluson was the writer or who created the material.

The two works transcribed onto newspaper in the early 13th Century just two years after Iceland was transformed to Christianity. In the process, the wealth of information regarding the Norse religion and mythology is likely to be lost for all time. The Eddas contain information from earlier sources and extend back to in the Viking Age. They are the principal source for The Icelandic skaldic tradition as well as Norse mythology.

The Eddic gods typically have a variety of names, which vary depending on the region. The most well-known ones include that of

Scandinavian as well as the Icelandic variations because of the abundance of information available from these regions. Naturally, one of the most important aspects of fascination in Norse mythology are the tales, adventures and struggles of gods and their connection to other Norse mythological creatures like the Jotunn, the Dwarves as well as the elves and, of course, humans. As with pantheons of other polytheistic societies the gods, goddesses and gods who starred in Norse mythology, had life-styles, emotions and flaws similar to the human race. They were dramatic, emotional were pranksters, played games and fell in love and even had children. Sometimes, they even perished as Baldr, godson of Odinn as well as Frigg.

Some Norse deities, like Loki, weren't worshipped. While Loki was a significant character in the Norse myths, there's no evidence of his followers in any way whatsoever. The geography of the area where a community resided dictated the way in which gods were worshipped and the way people dealt with them. It was believed that the Old Norse people considered the Norse gods to be their ancestors as well as acquaintances, not gods that they should be afraid of. While the Eddas offer a lot of information about Norse gods and their relationships with other races, Norse gods as well as their connections to other race, we aren't aware of what we know about Old Norse religious practices. There isn't much evidence to support this, and even though mentions of the religion are found in the Eddas however, it is crucial to note that the majority of sources used to examine Norse theology, mythology and religion were transliterated in the years after Christianity was introduced to Iceland in Iceland and Scandinavia. Therefore, it is possible that the stories were modified to be more closely resembling the Christian mythology.

While the writer for the "Prose Edda" was Christian and in the following paragraphs he argued that Heathens were swayed away to their "true faith," he insists that he attempted not to be a skeptic and kept the Edda as truthful as he could. He viewed the stories more as a form of art and an aid to Skalds in improving their pronunciation, rather than as a blatant "heresy." Whether he was honest about keeping the stories in their entirety is difficult to determine. There is no way to deny the similarities between the sacrificial hanging of Odinn and resurrection, as well as the crucifixion and the resurrection of Jesus Christ in the Christian mythology. That can be an indication of either "cross-contamination" or conscious alteration. In addition to the God stories, there's the Havamal an assortment that contains Old Norse poems that were oral transmissions in the Age of the Vikings. The poems were printed following the Christianization of Scandinavia and Iceland.

Magical Weapons in Norse Mythology

The myths about Norse mysterious weapons are known to have been muddled over time, but each weapon plays its own function. While many believe these five weapons of magic are identical, there is no link between the five weapons. Each represents five distinct features that are a part of Odin as well as Thor's perfect power and aren't all connected to one another.

Gram - Odin's Magical Sword

Odin is often portrayed using his sword Gram in battles against other gods. The hilt is gold with black runes engraved on it. The blade would be locked only when it was drawn by a person who was destined to beat Odin himself. Gram would then light up when held by its owner.

Gram was given the god Odin from the great Mimir and it gave him victory in numerous battles. Alongside the sword of Odin, it also served as the symbol of his power that's why he took it to combat along with his. Odin utilized his sword to battle one of his siblings Vili as well as Ve. In several versions of the mythological fight, Odin loses his eye and was replaced by a blood-red eye to represent the hurt he felt.

The sword was used in battles against Hoenir and Loki who snuck it out of the grasp of Odin by resembling their hands to Freya's. The Gram sword Gram cannot be broken however it can smash any sword it strikes. It is also often referred to as "Aegir's-bane," "Aegir" is Odin's father, the god of the sea and its stabbing power was the reason it was his weapon of choice.

Mjolnir - The Hammer of Thor

Mjolnir was created by Odin and was presented to Thor. It was made by combining two pieces that were forging hammers (Mjolnir) along with the handle (leggings). The hammer used for forging has the strength of lightning inside its head.

Handle is decorated by a dragon or snake figure , and it has a concealed compartment for an extremely powerful magic spell employed in the myth of Odin himself. This spell makes it the possibility to perform four magic spells at once.

Thor made use of his Hammer Mjolnir to shield gods against evil spirit and to stop the destruction of the world. Thor is described as fighting giants with it, however Thor never used it against human beings because Thor is against bloodshed and war. Thor also employed it to punish someone for committing a sin on him and his companions. When it is not in use the Mjolnir Hammer is stored in a special container beneath Odin's throne at Valhalla.

Gungnir - the Spear of Odin

Gungnir is the Spear of Destiny is believed to have been in the possession of Odin for a long time, from before the dawn of the time. It was created from the wood fragment that was thrown from Yggdrasil which is the life-giving tree that contains and connecting all the worlds. In accordance with the orders of Odin, Heimdall, the god's watchman put the timber upon Midgard (Earth) and then sorcery grew it into a huge tree which Heimdall donated his blood. Following Gungnir the spear was birthed, runes were cut into it to prevent anyone from being able to move it or harm Odin.

Gungnir is Odin's symbol that he employs to guard the gods. Odin employed this spear in order to bring down criminals as well as evil spirits who attack Asgard. In the event of conflict with humankind, Gungnir was launched in the direction of the gods and its power could eliminate all enemies. Gungnir is stored in a ring of metal (to which magic cannot be applied) which is where only Odin can reach it or look at it.

Gleipnir - Loki's Binding Cord

It is Loki's binding rope Gleipnir is a particular kind of ribbon that can be used to either tie someone down or let them go. It was created by dwarfs and then given to the gods to secure Loki in order to keep him from creating chaos.

It is made of the hair of the mare it is believed to have been utilized in some manner by every creature on earth, with some having positive and some with negative characteristics. Every hair is able to release or bind any creature it touches. Gleipnir is a synonym for the hair that can bind.

Dainsleif, the Sword of Thor

Dainsleif is the sword Thor employed to kill criminals and evil spirits. It was created by dwarfs by using a part of the Yggdrasil's heart. It was at Thor's disposal from at the very beginning, and was never stolen or lost. Dainsleif is thought to be among the strongest weapons of Asgard. It's easy to recognize due to its blade being nearly as long as three people.

These legendary weapons have become an integral part of our myths and legends , and provide inspiration for many stories. They also serve as a powerful depiction of Norse people's beliefs and culture. Many ways they represent their strengths as well as weaknesses gods.

Animistic Worldview

In putting animism in the context of other religions Some of the theological issues encountered in anthropology and religious history do not stem from the early connection of animism and an speculative idea of religious development, but rather from the wide range of animistic culture. As a model that is more broad than monotheism and polytheism and its definition is difficult to determine. It encompasses the beliefs of a majority within or from "small religions" but says nothing about their variety. In the end, other categories such as totemism shamanism, and ancestral propitiation are often employed.

In all likelihood they are not a representative of a person's entire religion. They are organizations that are not restricted to a single culture. Australian totemic cults bear the "family resemblance" to the African totemic cults despite their variations and differences are diverse. Shamanism, which is based upon the ecstasy of awe, can be traced back to Greenland to India and ancestor worship isn't restricted only to East Asia and Africa. The frequent appearance of groups of belief systems that conform to an established pattern suggests that there exist a few viable patterns and the basic principles of animism seem to be the primary reason for this. Animism places a lot of significance on the supernatural, which are distinct entities that are connected to specific locations and individuals or are in specific species and are independent by their relationships.

Every human encounter with the supernatural should be treated as a distinct event within the context of this system. While rituals may be a way to establish an ongoing moral connection with certain supernatural powers, people may be inclined to think of other sources of power they could choose to rely on in times of need. In times of stress the adherence to a particular god could change as gods were traded to tribal groups from Western Africa, and a desire to trade European products has led to an explosion of new cults of fundamentalists in Melanesia. The benefits of openness encourage the emergence of new ideas or a more eclectic approach to religion over charismatic chauvinism every time.

All animistic religions are required to communicate with supernatural beings, not only regarding moral issues or philosophy and more about practical issues like healing illnesses or securing food and staying clear of risk. It's common that true supernatural adoration isn't easy to find. Creator gods are often depicted in myths , but not in religious cults. The deceased are the most often portrayed as being part of ancient cults. The original clan ancestor, with all his symbolism is removed from both the community and godhead. If animistic powers exercise power everywhere, they do it in a specific, possibly self-centered way, penalizing people for the omission of a ritual or breaking taboos rather than acts of moral omission and violations of the secular.

The beliefs of the animal kingdom are difficult to blend into governmental systems, and will not be able to integrate with governmental systems in the future. If asked if the animism's connection to a smaller, less complex culture is evidence of its intrinsic (original) religious system, there is only one option that we don't know (and might never get) will be what panhuman that is, or prior to writing historical religion could have been similar to. The process of re-creating language from the beginning is a daunting task. If the term "spirituality" is used to describe an important system of interactions between human beings and the supernatural Societies without religion haven't been identified It is also possible to conclude that religion is the central point of a society, in which institutions' legitimacy is a factor.

The notion of supernatural spirits that animate all of nature regardless of regardless of whether these were gods fairies, shades or fates with whom humans could interact in meaningful ways, may be something from the past. Various theories assign traits of determination or reaction to the natural world. The individual's ability to perceive personal vision is being influenced by animistic beliefs throughout the world, which allows individuals to handle the issue on the basis of known the significance.

Chapter 6: The Values of Norse Paganism

The abundance of literary and historical sources from Norse mythology, it is clear to can see that pagans in the Northern Hemisphere followed an exemplary moral code. Viking or Icelandic Sagas as well as the Havamal The Poetic Prose Eddas, and the Havamal all contain mentions of this. Similar to others of the aspects they lived the morals of Norse people were also tied to gods. One of their best recognized values was the one that is now referred to in the form of"the" Nine Noble Virtues. The code of conduct is recognized and revered today by the adherents of the various forms of the modern Norse Paganism, including Asatru.

The Nine Noble Virtues of Asatru

Concerning the roots of these values, it's not easy to determine their origins. The people who shaped the modern-day Norse people generally didn't have a particular name for their religions. We know that their sources in literature provide common values as well as their relationship with Norse mythology. However, we do know we don't know the way they came to adhere to the Norse mythology. In addition to the core of the virtues listed the only other hint they provide the reader is that all adhered to the same religious beliefs. This lifestyle was among the most widely practiced religions for many thousands of years prior to the advent in Christianity within Europe.

While the beliefs associated with Norse paganism represent a distinct perspective, their adherents still strive to learn about the past Norse folk and ancient Nordic religion. In reviving the religionthat has roots dating back to the prehistoric period, they attempt to recreate the spiritual paths of the past Nordic people. Apart from the written record that are available, this process is assisted by archeological discoveries from the past in Scandinavia and Germanic regions. In addition, there are the oral legends and oral traditions which are still handed down to younger generations.

The core of every value is the human act. In accordance with these values one can alter their whole life only by changing their actions daily. Additionally the actions must be done to improve yourself and not to blindly following the actions of other people. But this doesn't mean that you do not need to adhere to the rules and laws of society in general. The goal of improving yourself is to be accomplished according to the following pattern: you are the first to make a difference in your own life and later, ultimately, in the lives of other people too. Although you may not be able to see this clearly when you perform a certain step, the reward will be revealed eventually to you.

Another essential aspect to think about is that you'll only see the results you create through a vigorous action. In other words it is impossible to make an improvement within your own life when don't take action on your own life. To actually begin, you must believe that it will happen. You must believe that you will be able and willing to take action to change. You must be convinced that if you are by doing the right things for yourself as well as for others honored by your choices. According to Asatru the reward you will receive will be a happier current life. This is quite different from other religions which offer only a lavish afterlife. Norse paganism allows you to make your own decisions about your happiness into the future as well as well as the happiness of those that surround you.

There is a major distinction between the beliefs of Norse paganism and the ethical code that is common to other religions. In particular, they do not have obscure concepts like atonement, sin, or penance that are commonly found in other religions--the Nine Noble Virtues of Asatru take on every single action that is either correct or incorrect. That means that if you're guilty of committing a sin you are responsible to rectify it and you don't need to apologize or hope for divine punishment, since they will not solve the problem. This is intended to make followers use their own minds and determine the best option for them. Being a human you possess a advanced mind and consciousness.

Although Northern gods instill these values by demonstrating them through the example of their personal lives, they can't be held accountable for the mishaps of others. In the end, it's your life and you are able to choose how you live it by analyzing your understanding of human values, such as respect, courage, honor or honesty. The quality of your life is able to be enhanced. Although different sources interpret these values in different ways but their core values always seem to be the identical. Each represents the same universal truth, which when followed can make one's life more efficient and appreciated by you and by others. They not only emphasize how important hospitality is, but moral and physical courage, and the most important thing integrity and honor, they are morally beneficial to live by.

The idea of the Nine Noble Virtues is considered to be a new concept, given that they were first codified through the Odinic Rite in England. But, at their core they represent the same values that were taught from the ancient Norse sources. Furthermore, they aren't only values cherished in the eyes of Old Norse people, nor are they strict rules to be followed. In essence, they're guidelines for how anyone must behave, or what kind of choices they can make throughout their lives. Most importantly, they will tell you how they should behave when faced by what happens as a result of actions.

Courage

Courage was an attribute given to warriors when they described their accomplishments physically. But, it's not always in the top spot on an impressive list of virtues due to another reason. Instead of being physically prepared to handle certain situations real courage refers to the moral capability to stand up for what's right even when you're faced with the disapproval of others. It's about standing up for your convictions when it's right. Because it usually requires a lot of courage and perseverance to achieve this, it's among the most important lessons you can take in Your Asatru experience. However keeping to these virtues requires a lot of determination.

If your friends are religiously conservative or stuck in their methods because they are unwilling to learn, establishing your own path could be difficult. In such a situation the level of spiritual power you'll require is likely to be similar to the physical power of Norse warriors. Courage doesn't mean that you're immune to fear of being rejected. It's a sign that you're confident enough to face these feelings and are able to express what's going on in your heart and mind, regardless of the possibility of refusal.

Truth

This should be obvious However, in some instances, speaking the truth could have negative results. But, doing so could be beneficial for your mental health as well as your relationships with others. Of course, there's huge difference between real fact and inner truth. If you aren't able to distinguish between the two and you're not able to talk about them. In general, the truth is what people accept and wishes to hear out loud. Contrary to that spiritual truth is the truth that you have in your heart to be real. It is common for people to be stuck just telling the first version because they want to be accepted within their circles of friends.

Finding out how to communicate your own beliefs about honesty is a task that requires an enormous amount of effort. It's much beyond simply not lying. Because what is widely accepted truth for others could be in fact a lie to you. Also, there's the possibility that you could effectively avoid telling lies when you do not engage in activities that you don't want others to ask questions about. If you do, don't discuss your secrets with those who don't have the same convictions that you have. If you don't, you might be enticed into lying in order to get rid of punishment, be it being excluded or any other.

Honor

Contrary to popular opinion Honorable means adhering to your own moral compass. This is the reason it's the basis in the system of values that is part of Norse paganism. Without honor, the other virtues will not be anything but a gimmick or be authentic. Your honor is the main reason you do what you do with every decision you make and your inner voice that will help you distinguish between right and wrong. If you rely on it, your name will be something that you can feel proud about. More importantly you'll be more at being content with yourself since the only way to gain respect from other people is to have built a strong sense of self-esteem.

Being able to feel a conviction to honor will not only help you, or those who surround you. Actually, it could influence the minds of future generations too. It's good to be recognized within your community as a moral person. Should something happen to you, it'd be a pleasant thought that you'll be remembered for these traits. By being an example to the younger generation, you will instill the same moral principles. This will improve their lives and they will be able to transfer this goodwill on to their children and the others they meet in their lives.

Fidelity

It is among the most intricate virtues that a human being could possess. It can mean keeping your faith or personal relationships or the community you belong to. All of them have the same significance in a person's life. This is the reason adhering to this principle can help you become the most successful person you could be. In the days of the early Norse people it was largely an issue of trust in the gods. The breaking of an oath could lead to causing offense to a god, and many times it was said to result in physical battles. Additionally, many adherents to Norse paganism still bind all other aspects of their faith to this primordial one.

In a world where people don't believe it's possible to remain true to your commitments anymore, sticking to your beliefs can open doors to a prosperous future. If people trust you as a person of faith and trustworthy, they'll trust you. This is the case even when they only are aware of one aspect about your personal life. If they know that you will stick to your word in one area they can be assured that you'll stick to your word in other areas too. This will help strengthen your relationships and enable you to build more.

Discipline

Discipline, or more precisely self-discipline is an essential quality to keep in mind. Being disciplined will provide you with the chance to promote other virtues too. An effective personal discipline that is reinforced will give you the capability to defend your beliefs as well as your moral code and many more. Adhering to these values must be your choice, one that you'll only be able make if you're strong enough to make it happen. If you're strong enough strong enough, you will be able to face any challenge, no matter if it's your own personal goal to overcome or not doing what people expect you to accomplish.

The task of keeping your standards up isn't easy due to all the temptations lurking all around us in our modern society and the multitude of people who want to exert their will over us. It can take years to perfect your self-control but it's well worth it. It will mean that you don't need to adhere to something that you do not want to adhere to or aren't convinced of. Additionally, it will show you how to get rid of any unnecessary issues in your life. One method to achieve this is to have the determination to place your trust in yourself. When you do this, you'll become less inclined to depend on other methods of emotional support. You will be a stronger person.

Hospitality

If we look at the history of any ancient civilization, we can see that the significance of hospitality was prominent in the creation of strong bonds within and outside of their environment. It was the same in the lives of Old Norse people either. Respecting different cultures and being open to other cultures was an essential element of life. Even though they were in families and groups, which were separated from each other they were open to everyone who came in. People who traveled were provided shelter and protection. In this way we must learn from the past. Nowadays, it is rare to offer shelter and food to anyone. However, just a few words of encouragement can improve someone's life.

In the modern world of technology We tend to separate our selves from the rest of the world. And more importantly, we forget to show respect and tolerance to different people. What can you do to be part of a community when you're unable to be certain aspects of it? The only way to be a respected part of any social group is to show equal respect to all of its members. Hospitality is more than just sharing your possessions in the end. It's about being a part of a community while keeping in mind the distinct characteristics that each person has in the group. A community will prosper is when everyone acts with respect and kindness.

Self-Reliance

Each of the Nine Noble Virtues can be achieved if you choose to decide to take the matter in your own hands. Even though the Norse gods can offer you general guidelines in life but you must be able to trust yourself more when making crucial decision. Only you are the one who can transform your lifestyle and take better choices for yourself. Naturally you'll only be able to achieve this if you take good care of yourself in both body and your mind. So, you can be sure to avoid blaming everyone and anyone else for your mistakes and accept responsibility to your own actions.

When it comes to self-reliance, there are times when you have to find the right equilibrium between trusting your own sense of self-reliance and relying on the advice of other people. If you're not able to learn to flourish as a person and as a person, you'll be unable to do the same within your community. You may also be inclined to not do things for others in order that you can make a profit. When you are able to depend on yourself, you'll be free of the lure of the lures of materialism and other lusts and vice versa. Norse people were not overly dependent on things of material value, and they valued possessions as a source of happiness and their purpose for their daily lives.

Industriousness

The same way, Norse people did not leave their tasks to fates of gods. You must also be aware of how important it is to work hard towards your goals. This is your obligation to the Norse gods as well as your family, friends, family members, and most importantly, you. In the past, physical labor was required to provide food for a table.

While in the present there are many ways to earn money in many other ways, you'll need to put in the effort to earn the same. It usually requires a lot of energy and time to achieve the goal you have set for yourself in life. But, if you're determined to reach your goal then you'll be able to conquer every obstacle that comes your way. You'll be able to use any method to accomplish this however, whatever you choose to do, don't be hesitant to the halfway point.

Perseverance

However hard you work, at times it is difficult to achieve because of all the obstacles life throws at you. When you are able to show perseverance, you'll be able to keep moving regardless of how dire the situation in front of you appears. Also, get up whenever you've fallen off your way to self-improvement Being determined will help you take lessons from the mistakes you made in the past. This serves the goal of showing everyone else that you are more successful as a person. In addition, there are the advantages it can bring to a community when each member is dedicated to improving their own lives and working in a team.

To achieve your maximum potential, you must have a firm determination to reach your goals. When the going gets tough and you're dissatisfied with yourself, it is the ideal moment to rise for the task and move ahead. If not, what else can you succeed? If you are able to blend your strengths through learning new abilities, you'll be successful in your life. The ancient Norse people survived through exactly this. They utilized all their abilities and were open to learning new ones, too. But most important they didn't give up regardless of what happened.

Magic in Norse Paganism

Magic was a significant element of Norse culture, and it encouraged many practitioners to engage in magic rituals and tricks, some of which were required to ensure prosperity for the Vikings. While we do not know much regarding Norse magic, numerous references regarding relevant practices and significant events offer a basic outline of what is necessary to comprehend the role of the magic of Norse pagan religions.

Branches of Norse Magic

Within the various subgroups of magical practices spa, seidr, galdr as well as runic magic comprised the main kinds of rituals practiced by professionals. While some had some similarities, the others were strictly an individual practice to maximize the benefits. Norse magic was performed by certain groups and cults, some of which were secret while others believed the practice to their work.

Seidr

The Iron Age that took place during the Late Scandinavian period gave rise to seidr magic that was linked with the future. Seidr practitioners utilized their abilities to either predict a individual's fate or to alter their future to achieve better results. Although some reports make connections between shamanism and seidr some believe that both are distinct practices that employ different techniques and rituals. While seidr magic was popular to both genders women, in particular were more adept in this technique. Numerous sorceresses were spotted performing seidr magic, as the practice was thought to be feminine.

The sorceresses were referred to as visendakona, seidkonur or volur. The males who practiced them were referred to as seidmenn. The word seidkonur refers to "black magician," which is the reason people stayed away from using the word. Instead, they preferred spa-kona, that brings another connotation to the light. In essence, both seidr and spa are distinct magical realms, each with its own characteristics as well as rituals and beliefs. This is why both terms were confusing for writers of later times. In essence "seidr" loosely refers "the act of binding" in that the word is translated to strings, cords, either halter or snare. Although the precise meaning of this term is uncertain, some refer to this practice as "spinning threads of fate." A few seidr-related practitioners utilized a device made from wool, strings and sticks to spin the distaff.

Seidr practitioners utilized humans as agents to communicate with gods and channel their inner voices to forecast the future. If the predictions weren't favorable, they used rituals that altered the movements of animals, and also to change the weather. The majority of magicians who performed seidr used their mind power to make illusions or to forget. It is important to note that seidr is no way of telling one's future using direct pictures or words, but rather communicating with gods and spirits to get clues about one's destiny. While some seidr enthusiasts came from the same clan they would often perform the rituals alone. But, some practitioners would practice magic in a group or with a couple of sisters.

As time passed, seidr began to take new forms and it was incorporated into various religious movements and some were used up until in the early 20th century. The practices that were based on seidr were classified by the term "magical-religious" movements that represented the modern Pagan rituals too.

Spa

The practice of magic was called spae, and was believed to be associated with the ability of personal gnosis, or intuition. It helped practitioners determine orlog, which is the rule of law, which is the manner in which entities were expected to behave. To determine if certain actions were legal spa professionals depended on their instincts. If not, they'd provide concrete solutions or suggestions to help you meet your objectives. The term volva can be interchangeably used in conjunction with Spa or orlog. In essence, the term volva refers to "Sybil" or "prophetess," which refers to a prophetess or witch along and her team.

When the Norns played with fortunes through the threads, and called on the higher spirits to determine what would happen to all living beings the volva could see the future of a person in the situation or the creature they chose. The literal meaning for "volva" in the Old Norse language is "the carrier of magic" or the "wand carrier." According to some sources that a volva was awe-inspiring knowledge and could use it to predict the future. The volva was revered by all gods and people. Indeed some of Norse stories tells of Odin looking into the eyes of a volva, in order to discover his fate, along with other Aesir gods.

Certain practitioners of spae magic utilized their skills to read the stories of their ancestors. They could be able to determine their future. Women who used spae magic were revered for their ability to assist nobles make the right decisions by anticipating the future. They could play an important role in the planning of war and offer insights to alter motives to win. They would also provide insight into the motivations of war. Veleda was a renowned prophetess who predicted victory of her army as well as the Batavi army, which fought the Romans. In keeping with the traditional Germanic practices, Veleda's abilities were often compared to god's, making her respected and respected in that time.

Women and men were mainly members of the spae magician community. In comparison to the seidr followers The spae group was considered to be more valuable since they could predict the future with accuracy. They offered more detail and were part of prestigious clans and families. Spae magic was comprised of a variety of techniques which were employed according to the situation and needs. While the majority of methods were based on trance-like effects, some also involved singing certain mantras and words that linked everything. As an example, the Thorgeirr The Lawspeaker was a well-known spae operator who was commissioned to forecast Iceland's future, based on the beliefs of religion. Because of the volume demands, he fled from his followers and then allegedly disappeared "under the cloak."

Runic Magic

Runic magic is the art of decoding and reading "runes," or phonetic characters from the time of the Norsemen. They were believed to be magical and the inscriptions that were relevant to them conjured the spectre of curses as well as blessings. The ones who knew the correct method to read the runes had a lot of power. From predicting the outcome of a person's fate to forecasting their destiny The runes could help one to change their life. Certain runic inscriptions were created to safeguard the stone or stone. In the case of this inscription people were warned of the calamity that could strike those who dared take the stone away. This means that the runes could be the catalyst to determine the future of a person.

In the majority of cases, runic inscriptions that fall into the wrong hands will be destructive and ruin the person's life. Thus, reading and handling the runes was a honed skill. Certain runes were also utilized to treat ailments or improve health through internal healing. The existence of runes isn't explicit within any of the Old Norse tales. However, there are stories that refer to Odin being hung from the Yggdrasil, in order to discover more about runes and the art of studying them. In the final moments before his death, he managed to get the runes in his hands and returned to his former self.

Certain documents associated with skaldic poetry describe runsic formulas that are magical, hidden songs, and hidden skills that required a specific skill to unravel. This led to the development of runic magic. The practitioners employed their talents to decode the runic inscriptions and predict the future of a person. In some instances, certain ailments could be treated by using runic magic. Practitioners who were skilled in runic magic utilized it to satisfy their desires, heal emotional wounds, ease the agitation and even comprehend animal communication.